MISS PIGGY'S
GUIDE TO LIFE

Miss Piggy's Guide to Life

by MISS PIGGY

as told to Henry Beard

Muppet Press/Alfred A. Knopf

1 9 8 1

New York

THIS IS A BORZOI BOOK
PUBLISHED BY THE MUPPET PRESS AND
ALFRED A. KNOPF, INC.

Library of Congress Cataloging in Publication Data

Main entry under title: Miss Piggy's guide to life.

1. American wit and humor.
PN6162.M53   1981   818'.5402   80-2708
ISBN 0-394-51912-4   AACR2

Manufactured in the United States of America

FIRST EDITION

This Book Is Dedicated to
Kermit
My Life, My Love, My Frog

♥　♥　♥

Contents

♥ ♥ ♥

Les Acknowledgments

Moi would like to take this opportunity to thank all the nice people who worked so hard on this book: that cute John E. Barrett, who took all the wonderful pictures of moi (he *is* fortunate to have such a stunning subject); dear, sweet Calista Hendrickson, moi's personal stylist and costume designer, who was so very helpful in adding all those countless teensy bits of polish and gloss to my *Guide to Life;* those charming, marvelous prop men, Dennis Smith and Bruce Morozko, who created and helped conceive for moi all the very many backgrounds, settings, and accessories that help accentuate moi's natural loveliness; darling Deborah Lombardi, my talented and gifted costumeur; divine, priceless Amy Koblenzer, who supervised and coordinated the entire production of this—if moi does say so, and moi *does*—remarkable volume; those lovely and invaluable ladies, Marianne Bernstein, Photographer's Assistant, Debbie Schneider, Stylist and Prop Assistant, and Lynden Mosse, Production Assistant; Cathy Canzani, for those lovable graphs; moi's favorite Art Directeur, Michael K. Frith (so distinguished looking!), who was a great help in many, many stages of this projequete; adorable Bobby Gottlieb, my Editeur and Publischere (*so* très, très gallant, and *so* interested in ballet!); Knopf's ravissante book designer, Virginia Tan, with her cute little colored pencils and sharp little scissors and pots of sticky rubber cement; my Editorial Directeur, the very lovely and dedicated Jane Leventhal or Whatever-her-name-is (such phone bills!); my long-time ami Christopher Cerf, who contributed oodles of good ideas (most of which I would have thought of myself if I had not been *so* busy); my oldest, dearest friend and associate, Frank Oz, who has been so supportive over the years and to whom moi owes so much in moi's development as a superstar; and last, but not least-esse, Moi Moiself, without whom all of the people on this list would probably be doing something very boring and unrewarding in the appliance field in Delaware.

Introduction

Call me Moi . . .

I have always believed that moi had great natural gifts as a writeur, and so one day not long ago I decided to answer the call of my Muse. Well, that is a bit of what we in the word biz call poetic license. Actually, I answered an ad on the back of a matchbook that said "If You Can Write a Check, You Can Write a Book."

Ah, but I must caution you, dear fan, admirer, or other, I did not embark lightly on a literary career! It is a very demanding craft, and I know, as only an autheur can, what long and lonely hours must be spent in careful preparation before so much as a single adverbative or dejective is set to paper!

I have lost count of the days I have devoted to finding the perfect writing outfit (a pale blue silk blouse, pearl-gray pleated skirt, and a simple pillbox hat); the correct writing instrument (a nice gold ballpoint pen with a little lever on the side that lets you pick any of six colors of ink depending on your mood); and a comfortable, appropriate writing desk (a unique Murray XIVth scribbloire).

Plays, verses, epic poems, heroic couplets, and the shorter crosswords are my true métier, but when at last I had a few precious moments to give to my art, I thought first and foremost of my millions of fans. What, I asked moiself, do *they* need? The answer was as quick as it was speedy: a guide. And not just any guide, but a Guide to Life.

Oh, how often in those early, hard years, before I became the superstar I was destined to be, have I wished for a book exactly like the one you are holding in your hand—a simple, clear volume with lots of pictures of moi and all the right answers to every important question!

And I knew that if ever such a book came along, I would not merely riffle through it, as perhaps you are now doing, but instantly rush over to the counter and buy it for fear that such a treasure would slip from my grasp.

"Here at last is just the book I have been looking, even pining, for," I would cry to the salesperson. "It is woven from the very fabric of life itself!

It has heart, soul, body, shine, and bounce. It is a kiss on the hand, a port in a storm, a seat on the aisle! Huzzah! I'll take it!"

And if an ill-informed bookseller attempted to convince me to substitute for it some flossy novel about sad people in big houses by a woman with three names, I would reject it politely but without hesitation. "Take back your flossy novel about sad people in big houses by a woman with three names," I would insist, indicating with a quick movement of my hand in what contempt I held such trash.

And then, helping him up from the floor, I would ask him in the nicest possible way to wrap up my *Guide* in some pretty gift paper, for I would consider it a great gift from the autheur to moi, as, in fact, this little book is a gift from moi to toi.

And toi are very welcome!

Miss Piggy
xx

MISS PIGGY'S
GUIDE TO LIFE

Beauty

Beauty. Such a short, simple word, and yet, cher readeur, how much mystery, enchantment, and just plain fuss those six letters contain! But what *is* beauty? And how can you achieve it?

In a word, beauty is being yourself. (After all, if people really could be someone else, everywhere you looked there would be millions of moi!) Start with what you are—not with what you wish you were or what those silly magazines tell you you ought to be. Then add those dozens of teensy little touches that bring out the beauty that's already there.

Believe it or not, most great beauties were not born beautiful. Of course, there are always a few conventional pretty faces who find their way onto soap packages and into bug spray ads, but they lack that inner depth, that unique style that is shared by women (like moiself) who have made themselves beautiful. Quick, try to call to mind the most recent Miss America winner. *Any* Miss America winner. You can't? I didn't think so (frankly, neither can I). But now try to picture Lauren Bacall. Or Katharine Hepburn. Or moi. You see? I rest my case.

Naturally, it is not easy to become beautiful. It requires hard work, patience, and attention to detail. It also takes a certain firmness of purpose. Beauty is in the eye of the beholder, and it may be necessary from time to time to give a stupid or misinformed beholder a black eye.

Ah, but beauty is worth the effort! Yes, there is the terrible pressure that comes with being the object of so much attention, of so many adoring fans, but there is also the satisfaction of providing your public with a vision of true beautology, true stylisity—how can I put it?—true *glamorositude,* in a world that can sometimes seem, well, a little on the gray side.

Now, not everyone can be a superstar, but anyone can be a semistar, a starette, or a teensyweensystar. The most important thing is to believe that you are beautiful. If, when you start out, you don't get immediate results, don't be discouraged. For one thing, beauty takes practice. But, more important, often the only view we have of ourselves is from a mirror or a photograph. Due to defection, refaction, conflection, and infliction, mirrors always make you look larger in the wrong places. (An important scientist at a big university in a famous place discovered this.) And cameras *do* lie, because of all kinds of strange optical things and complicated gizmos that break and give you the wrong shortstop or spoil the focus-pocus and little hairs that get stuck inside and goo on the film. (After all, camera lenses are more like a fly's eye than our own, and who cares what some nasty little insect thinks you look like, anyway?)

My advice is, follow my advice: Never forget that only *you* can ever fully appreciate your own true beauty. Others may try, but they so often fall short.

First Things First : Rating Your Beauty Assets

Before you can set yourself the goal of becoming beautiful, you must take a good look at yourself, and then make a frank list of your pluses and minuses. Be honest with yourself (of course, you needn't go overboard). If you start out with an exaggerated sense of your current appearance, you may miss wonderful opportunities to make dramatic improvements.

Take a look at the beauty audit I did for myself to get an idea of the various areas you should pay attention to.

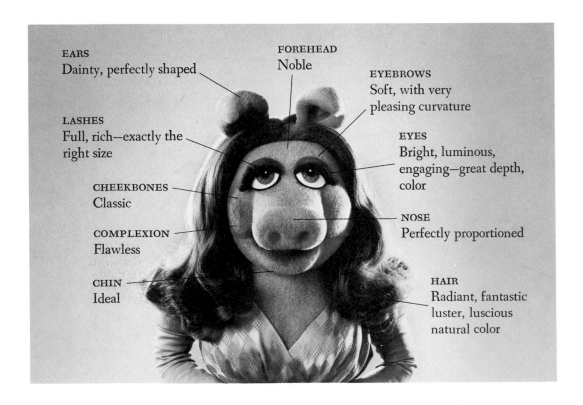

EARS
Dainty, perfectly shaped

FOREHEAD
Noble

EYEBROWS
Soft, with very pleasing curvature

LASHES
Full, rich—exactly the right size

EYES
Bright, luminous, engaging—great depth, color

CHEEKBONES
Classic

COMPLEXION
Flawless

NOSE
Perfectly proportioned

CHIN
Ideal

HAIR
Radiant, fantastic luster, luscious natural color

Divide your Beauty Zone into Areas of Concentration (things to work on) and Areas of Commendation (things to congratulate yourself on having already). On an itsée-bitsée piece of paper, make a list of what you want to change and put it somewhere out of sight but handy. On a very large piece of paper, make a list of what you're happy with. Stick it on your mirror. Now you're ready to begin.

Face Facts

There are two kinds of complexion: Problem and Perfect. I am fortunate to have the latter. But, if you're one of the many, many people with a Problem Complexion, this list contains everything you need to know to put your best face forward.

Problem	*Solution*
Spots	Spot remover
Splotches	Mop, then wax and buff
Wrinkles	Smooth with teensy steamroller
Crow's feet	Wear little scarecrow earrings
Bags under eyes	Fold and put away in pantry
Dimples	Remark that Greta Garbo had dimples
Oil	Dip face in troubled water
Dry skin	Sprinkle morning and evening
Facial hair	Read ghost story, then clip
A great deal of facial hair	Consider circus career
Dull skin	Take face for ride on roller coaster
Rough skin	Avoid rough foods like celery, potato skins, and shredded wheat. Stick to soft, silken foods—cream, chocolate sauce, mashed potatoes
Redness in eyes	Eliminate sad movies until condition passes

But even if you have a Perfect Complexion, you do need to maintain it. A few minutes a day is all it takes, thanks to my unique "face-saving" method.

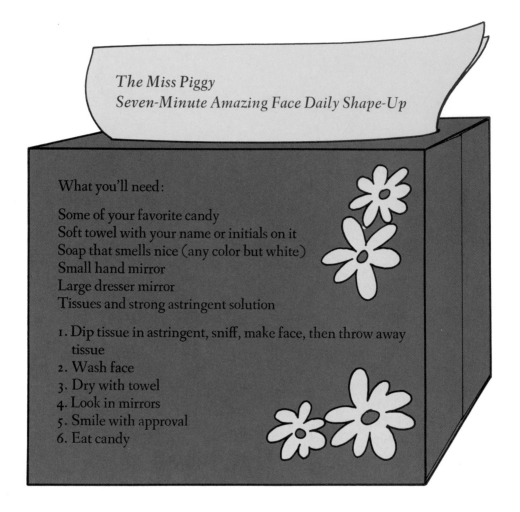

The Miss Piggy
Seven-Minute Amazing Face Daily Shape-Up

What you'll need:

Some of your favorite candy
Soft towel with your name or initials on it
Soap that smells nice (any color but white)
Small hand mirror
Large dresser mirror
Tissues and strong astringent solution

1. Dip tissue in astringent, sniff, make face, then throw away tissue
2. Wash face
3. Dry with towel
4. Look in mirrors
5. Smile with approval
6. Eat candy

FEEDING YOUR FACE

It's a good idea to apply an allover facial pack about once or twice a month to keep skin tone robust, but I never, never use mud (frankly, it brings up unpleasant memories). I prefer and recommend my own special facial mousse, a mixture of mocha, cooking chocolate, confectioners sugar, eggs, and cream (adjust the proportions to your own taste). The mousse should be beaten with an eggbeater and applied with a wooden spatula just as if you were frosting a cake. If there's a little left over, it is quite all right to taste a teensy bit of it.

You Need Hair to Be Great

Your hair is your most important accessory. In a pinch, you could do without your shoes, your purse, your jewelry—even your eye shadow—but without your hair, in that all-important first impression you'd score a Bad Beauty Impact.

And yet, so many women take their hair for granted. They treat it as if it is just a chore—something to be washed, dried, and put away. They don't have hair-dos, they have hair-didn'ts.

Having a dull hairstyle is like putting an olive on top of a chocolate sundae. It makes your whole appearance unappetizing.

Hair isn't a hat you just happened to grow. It is a golden opportunity for the fullest possible expression of your personality. Don't wear the same drab hairstyle day after dreary day. Experiment!

I find that this country-and-western coiffure nicely expresses my rural roots and my simple philosophy of personal loyalty—I Stand By My Frog.

Not every occasion calls for an elabo-rate hairstyle solution. Here I have adopted a simple tease with a little bit of fashion accenting to wear on a teensy errand to pick up some dry cleaning.

The traditional demure Japanese geisha look fits me to a ceremonial "T." Kissu-kissu!

Sometimes I just *have* to go incognito to get away from my millions of admirers. This appealing disguise preserves my anonymity from all but a few hundred of the most alert columnists, photographers, and truly dedicated fans.

The recent fad for this rather extreme style has made it a little "Bo-ring," but it is a nice change of pace. As you can see, I am an eleven.

For a really effective nostalgia look, it's "bangs for the memories." The styles of the twenties suit me particularly well, don't you think so? I SAID, DON'T YOU THINK SO! Oh, you do? How sweet!

What hairstyle is best for you? Ma chérie, *any* hairstyle is best for you as long as you don't wear it self-consciously. If you walk around looking as though someone dumped something on your head, your manner will undercut the very effect you're trying to create.

The same goes for wigs. If you act as if there's a poodle on your noodle, no wig will ever work for you. Here is a teensy piece of advice that may help the first time you change your usual style to something more exciting (or when you're wearing something particularly daring). Put a bit of spinach on a tooth and smile a lot. You would be amazed how effective this is in taking an enormous amount of otherwise unnerving attention away from your new hair-do.

Needless to say, the few hairstyles I have demonstrated in this chapter represent only a fraction of my beauty repertoire, but they should show you what I have in mind. Of course, in order to adapt to any style effortlessly, and to display that rich shine that is always so appealing, moi's hair needs body, and so I make sure that my hair gets the essential nutrients it needs at least once a week. Follow this simple hair-care technique, and when you let your hair down, it won't let *you* down.

Miss Piggy's Petite Coiffure
Style-and-Smile Hair Conditioning Recipe

2 tsp butter	⅓ cup sugar
1 tbsp flour	3 egg yolks
1 cup milk	1 tsp vanilla
1 oz powdered chocolate	3 egg whites

1. Heat the milk, sugar, and chocolate, beat in the yolks, then whip in the vanilla and the egg whites. Place in the oven on very low heat.

2. Go out and have your hair done.

3. Come home, remove mixture from oven, cover lightly with whipped cream, and eat.

Makeup Rules I Made Up—Don't Break Them!

With so many different kinds of cosmetics and so many different types of coloring, shading, and toning that can be achieved by using them, there simply is no one correct makeup method. What's right for moi may not be right for you (for example, you probably use a little less ear-liner). However, what is *wrong* for moi is definitely wrong for you, too. Consult my Ten Tone Commandments. If you avoid these makeup sins, chances are your appearance will be heavenly.

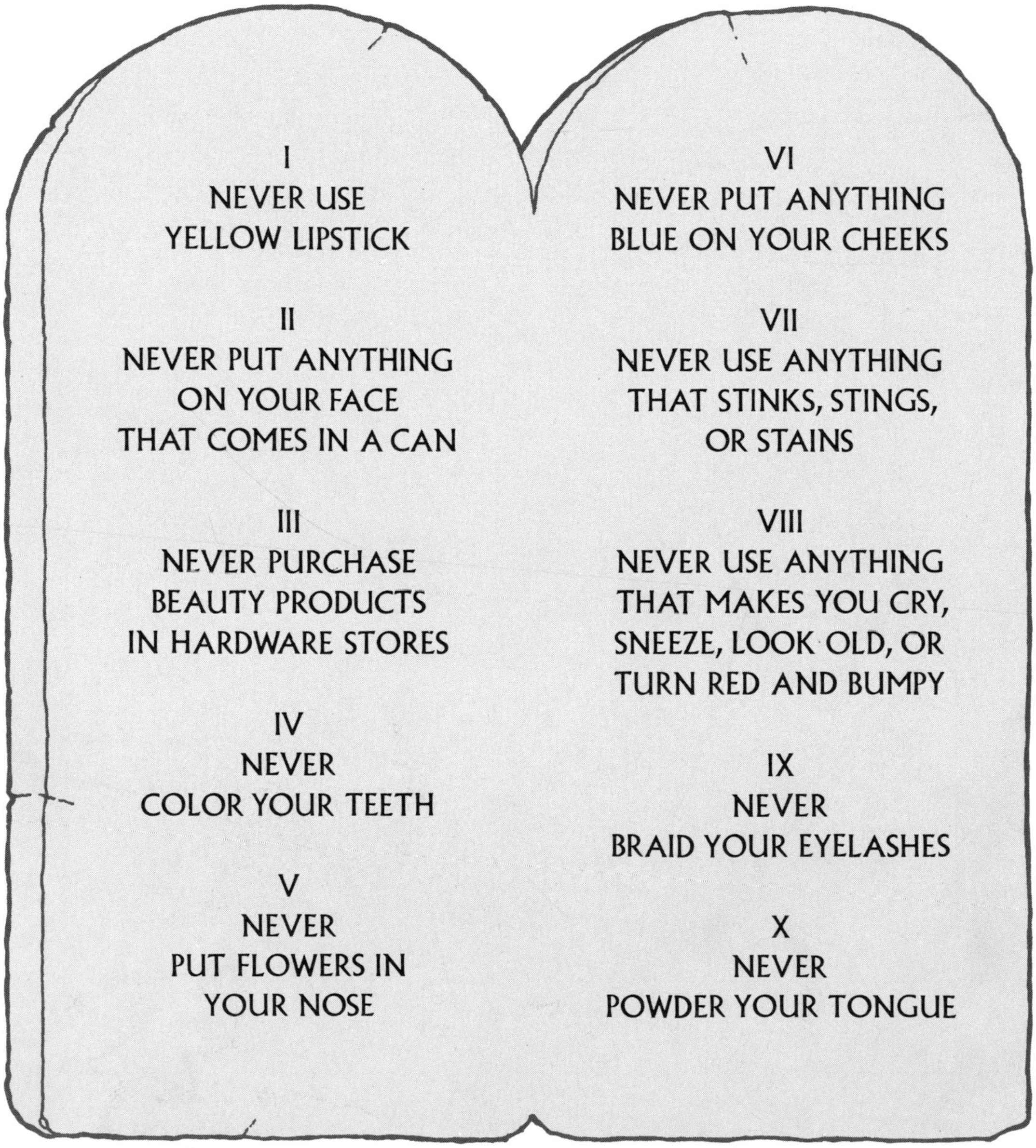

I
NEVER USE
YELLOW LIPSTICK

II
NEVER PUT ANYTHING
ON YOUR FACE
THAT COMES IN A CAN

III
NEVER PURCHASE
BEAUTY PRODUCTS
IN HARDWARE STORES

IV
NEVER
COLOR YOUR TEETH

V
NEVER
PUT FLOWERS IN
YOUR NOSE

VI
NEVER PUT ANYTHING
BLUE ON YOUR CHEEKS

VII
NEVER USE ANYTHING
THAT STINKS, STINGS,
OR STAINS

VIII
NEVER USE ANYTHING
THAT MAKES YOU CRY,
SNEEZE, LOOK OLD, OR
TURN RED AND BUMPY

IX
NEVER
BRAID YOUR EYELASHES

X
NEVER
POWDER YOUR TONGUE

BEFORE

There is absolutely no one who is such a total wreck that he can not be made into a picture of demure loveliness with the conscientious application of my basic beauty principles. Just to illustrate that point, I selected as my subject an individual whose appearance was so repulsive I had to have my mirrors insured. Look at this character. It seems hopeless, no?

AFTER

Voilà! A total, top-to bottom transformation. A few simple, subtle changes have turned a truly desperate case into a fashion plate. The key to a successful make-over is knowing what to accentuate and what to play down. Although in this instance the simplest course would have been to play down the individual by placing a white sheet over the entire figure and play up the wall or maybe a piece of furniture, I wanted to demonstrate to you that even the most challenging beauty problem can be solved by tastefully emphasizing the positive and concealing the negative.

THAT TAN-TALIZING BEACHES-AND-CREAM COMPLEXION

To develop a soft, rich, bronze-goddesse tan, moi sunbathes during the summer months. I do have to watch out for my Kermie, though. If he gets even a teensy bit blue, I know it's time to head for the shade.

It's Scentsational!

Perfume is a subject dear to my heart. I have so many favorites: Arôme de Grenouille, Okéfénôkée, Eau Contraire, Fume de Ma Tante, Blast du Past, Kermès, Je Suis Swell, and Attention S'il Vous Plaît, to name a few. But here again, it's a matter of personal taste, and so I will confine myself to giving you:

Answers to the Three Most-Often Asked Perfume Questions

How much?	A lot
Where?	All over
When?	Any time

A Few Last Bon Mots

Sadly, many women think beauty is something they can buy, and if only they were rich, they could be gorgeous. Phooey. Beauty isn't being able to shop in fancy stores where it looks like they put phone numbers on the price tags by mistake, and you have to empty your wallet to buy something in a bottle the size of a gumdrop.

Now, I am not saying that you shouldn't splurge once in a while and treat yourself to something that makes you look or smell fabulous. You should—after all, you deserve it! But don't think beauty lives in your purse. It doesn't, it lives in your heart. Take it from one who knows. After all, the best thing in my life that's green isn't money. . . .

Body Language

Moi speaks body language fluently (although with a slight French accent), and I find it so helpful in getting my emotional points across. What is body language? Quite simply, it is all the teensy gestures, facial expressions, and postures people use to communicate their inner feelings.

It is very important to pay attention to these little signs and signals, because someone may be saying something very sweet to you but at the same time be putting a nasty rubber spider in your purse. Or a dear friend might appear just a bit standoffish, and you could mistake his seeming coolness for a lack of interest and fail to notice the deep longing in his eyes and the flush of blazing romantic passion that slowly creeps over his green—well, you get the idea.

Take a look at these typical examples of body language:

Letting the Chat Out of the Bag

If ...	The hidden meaning is ...
A friend stands with folded arms, tapping his feet, as you arrive a teensy bit late—	"Heck, how does that tune go? Dum DEE DUM? DUM dee dee DEE?"
Someone you are telling a story to keeps looking at his watch—	"Isn't it amazing how fast time passes when you are having a really good time?"
A person you are talking to suddenly frowns, squints, and grimaces all at the same time—	"You are standing on my foot."
An acquaintance forgets your name—	"I do not place a high value on my relationship with you."
An acquaintance forgets *moi's* name—	"I do not place a high value on my life."

Talking Turkey

Body language can provide a handy means of delicately raising a subject which it would be unladylike to address directly. Let us say that you wish to be taken out to dinner, but your prospective dining companion is a little slow on the uptake, and you are becoming quite hungry. As you pursue some innocuous conversational topic like the weather, you construct this simple "secret" sentence: "I" (point to yourself) "am famished" (rub tummy) "and would like to go out and eat" (knife and fork motions, with a little chewing). "Your" (point to companion) "treat" (rub first two fingers and thumb together). If all else fails, fake a fainting spell and mutter "food, food" in a delirious sort of way.

Gab for Gifts

It is also not polite to come right out and ask someone to purchase something for you, but you can get your point across very effectively without your friend being any the wiser with a deft use of body language. Suppose you are shopping, and you have spotted a nice pair of earrings. Stop for a minute or two and stare directly at them, and then, daintily touching an earlobe with each hand, say, "There is a RINGING in my EARS. It will probably pass BUY AND BUY, but right now it is the GOLD-darnedest sensation. It came on as suddenly as a PUNCH IN THE NOSE." As if by magic, your friend will immediately offer to purchase the earrings for you.

Beauty Language

As an actresse, I have no difficulty in conveying the whole range of emotions from A to high C, and I can employ my rich vocabulary of physical expression to touch people (quite hard, if necessary) in ways that mere language cannot. Peruse these (stunning) photographs of moi and note how effectively I can converse on a very personal level without saying a single word.

1. "Here moi is—tender, vulnerable, alluring."

2. "But also full of passion, romance, and a delicious ice cream sundae I had an hour ago."

3. "Have you something nice to give me? Do you not think that would be a good idea? Hmmmm?"

4. "I urge you to consider my needs as a person very carefully."

5. "And very quickly."

6. "Oh, I cannot guess what it is!"

7. "How sweet, how thoughtful, how prudent!"

8. "I shall treasure this teensy hanky for a reasonably long period of time, for although it certainly does not look like it set you back much, the feeling it expresses is beyond price."

Depressed?

How to Cope with What Makes You Mope

The basic trouble with depression is that it is so depressing. You see, even if you started out in a *good* mood, you would get gloomy if all you did was sit in a chair in your dressing room with the shades pulled down watching afternoon television. But when you are already in a lousy frame of mind, you just make yourself unhappier and unhappier, and the sadder you get, the less you feel like doing anything that would cheer you up. It is what psychiatrists call a fishous circle (I think they call it that because you feel the way goldfish must feel, going around in circles in those teensy bowls, looking at that stupid little castle all day and nibbling on stuff that looks like sawdust).

Your Blessing Census

It often helps to look on the bright side. Make a teensy list of things that have not happened that really *would* be depressing if they had. Here is one of moi's:

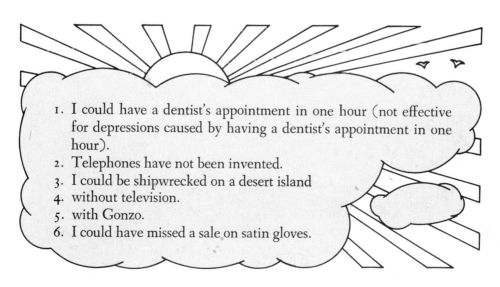

1. I could have a dentist's appointment in one hour (not effective for depressions caused by having a dentist's appointment in one hour).
2. Telephones have not been invented.
3. I could be shipwrecked on a desert island
4. without television.
5. with Gonzo.
6. I could have missed a sale on satin gloves.

Sad Snacks

Just because you are down in the mouth, that is no reason not to eat. For one thing, you may be suffering from one of a large number of very specific medically guaranteed forms of depression caused by an unfulfilled longing for a certain food, like watermelancholy, caramelancholy, and lemonmeringuecholy, or chocolochondria, petit-fourlornness, tartache or flanguish.

And even if it is not one of these that is ailing you, having a nice meal with a candle and a flower on the table—or just a little "candy-depressant" —is one of the easiest and most effective ways to cure the blues. Warning: don't put together some miserable-looking snack of horrid things from the back of the refrigerator. There is nothing worse than a meal of such depressing foods as soft lettuce, dusty peanuts, and canned tongue.

Bubble That Bathos Away!

You can often wash your troubles away with the right kind of bath. Throw everything you have into the tub: bubble gels, bubble oils, bubble powders, bubble gum. And speaking of bubbles, why not have a lovely glass of champagne within easy reach?

How to Be Your Own Best Fan

Whenever you are really down, just sit in front of your mirror, and remind yourself of all your talents and accomplishments and successes. When you have examined things reasonably, you will find that you have nothing to be depressed about at all. Anyway, that's the idea. Good luck!

Misery Loves Timpani

If your depression is particularly acute, you may be able to deglumify things a bit with some upbeat music. But if you like classical music—as moi does—do be careful: even the most sprightly, toe-tapping symphonies have at least one grouchy movement filled with oboes, doldrums, and bassinets.

And stay away from sourpuss composers whose names begin with a "D," like Dostoevsky and Debussy. All they ever wrote was stuff like "Pavane for a Swan Who Got Run Over by a Truck." (Personally, I think the works of Anton Musak make very pleasant listening.)

When It's Grim, Don't Bare It

When you are depressed, you should keep it to yourself. Even if I have to drag myself out of my chair, I answer the phone in a cheery voice as if nothing were bothering me. "You sound a little down," says Kermie. I reply, "Who, *moi*? My goodnesse, *whatever* gave you *that* idea? Why, I am as happy as a clam who just landed the lead in 'Singing Shellfish.' And how are *you*?" After this cheery exchange I drag myself back to my chair and return to my joyless thoughts. My mind wanders to the mudslides, avalanches, and cyclones that put regular shipments of lip gloss in peril each and every day. Perhaps right now the lip gloss train is being plunged into an abyss by a freak meteor bath! Oooooooooooh.

Yet no matter how bad things may seem, it is always better in the morning. I may cry myself to sleep, but next matin, I jump out of bed, throw open the curtains, and say, "The sun is shining, the birds are singing, and I am so lucky to be moi—Au Revoir, Sadnesse!"

Diet

There is no *one* diet to follow all the time. Superstars such as moiself use a number of different dieting methods to maintain the trim, slim figure that pleases fan and frog alike.

In this chapter, I am presenting a week of diet dinners, Sunday through Friday. (When you are following as strict a regimen as the one I am outlining here, it is really quite all right to splurge once a week. Thus, there is no diet dinner for Saturday.)

The Diet of Diets

This diet is in many ways my favorite. It is flexible, and it provides a wide variety of different dishes to choose from. Here is how it works. Get six or eight of the most interesting-looking diet books, pick the most appetizing recipes from each, and organize them into meals.

For example, one noted diet makes you eat an awful lot of grapefruit, a fruit I find about as appealing as a beach ball. And yet that very same diet lets you eat chocolate cake and non diet sodas.

Another popular weight-loss regime forbids desserts of any kind, but actually encourages you to eat your fill of french fries, ravioli, and quiche.

Now, either of these diets by itself would be impossibly vile, but careful selection of the best offerings from each gives you the following low-calorie feast:

Sunday

Small Quiche Appetizer
Ravioli with French-Fried Potatoes
Chocolate Cake à la Mode
Very Large Cola Drink

The Hidden Diet

A very common oversight in most weight-limitation programs is to pay excessive attention to the calories you consume rather than to the enormous numbers of calories you routinely avoid.

Let's take a look at two dinners. The first is what I call the Basic Maximum Possible Dinner. I am including it here on my diet for purposes of comparison only, and I certainly do not recommend it as part of this diet, except of course as a possible Splurge.

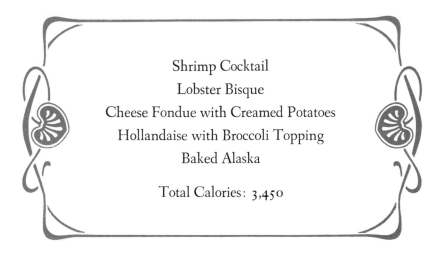

Shrimp Cocktail
Lobster Bisque
Cheese Fondue with Creamed Potatoes
Hollandaise with Broccoli Topping
Baked Alaska

Total Calories: 3,450

The second dinner is a more prudent—and clearly far more typical—meal and I call that the Standard Regular Normal Dinner. It is the next day's offering in my Weight-Conscious Week.

Monday

Three Slices of Pizza
Double Scoop of Ice Cream with Topping de Choice
Soft Drink

Total Calories: 1,250

As you can readily see, it is only the second day of your diet, and you have saved over 2,000 calories! Keep up the good work!

The High-Activity Diet

There are a few foods—mostly quite unpleasant ones, I am sorry to say—which require the expenditure of more calories to eat than they actually contain. Celery and cabbage are the best-known comestibles in this category.

However, it is hardly necessary to limit yourself to tasteless stalks and leaves that you need a pair of pliers to help you chew in order to obtain exactly the same kind of benefit. What moi does, at least once a week, is to choose a fairly distant restaurant—one several blocks away—and go there to eat. Let's see how those calories melt away, for the most part *in advance* of the actual meal:

Applying makeup	25	Entering restaurant and sitting down at table	9
Looking for purse	30	Moving to a better table	4
Looking for shoes	15	Lifting and reading menu	3
Closing door	5	Eating	12
Going back inside to get the key	6	Checking the bill	3
Checking for mail on the way out	3	Polite discussion with waiter	5
Opening envelope	2	Figuring the tip	2
Tearing up bill	8	Figuring the tip again	2
Walking to restaurant: Up and down 8 curbs @ 1 calorie per curb	8	Looking in the bottom of my purse for that five I know is down there somewhere	15
Checking for traffic (both ways) at 8 intersections @ 1 calorie per intersection	8	Return trip	26
Carrying purse for 15 minutes	10	Total Expended Calories	298

And now let's look at the meal I had:

Tuesday

Salad with French, Russian, and Roquefort Dressing, Croutons, and Grated Cheese		175
Bread and Butter		125
Seafood á la Newburg		200
Rice		100
String Beans	(tasted awful)	0
Applie Pie à la Mode		90
		925
Total Calorie Intake After Subtracting Total Expended Calories		342

Amazingly enough, the net result is exactly the same as it would have been if I had stayed at home and eaten nine slices of protein toast. And it was a great deal more fun!

The Hunger-Impulse Diet

The trouble with so many diets is that they ignore a very simple fact: people eat because they are hungry, and they overeat because they are extremely hungry. Thus, the worst possible way to attempt to control your weight is by missing meals.

This fundamental principle can be applied quite effectively to dieting. Do you remember how your parents would say, "Don't fill up on those [whatever they were], you won't be able to finish your dinner"?

Well, if in fact your aim is not to finish your dinner—or, to put it another way, to have just a teensy, diet-conscious meal—you can snack your way to the weight you desire by nipping hunger in the bud whenever it appears.

Wednesday

4:14 p.m.	Two cookies
4:34	One more cookie
4:51	Small handful of peanuts
5:17	Slightly larger handful of peanuts
5:44	The rest of the peanuts
6:11	Crackers with cheese dip
6:32	Breadstick with cheese dip
6:45	Cheese chips with cheese dip
7:10	Small slice of cake from piece left in icebox
7:26	Remainder of cake (really, it is silly to have such a small piece on a big plate taking up so much room)
7:38 p.m.	One peanut-butter-and-jelly sandwich
7:42	With potato chips
7:46	And two pickles
8:01	Another cookie
8:11	Remainder of dip on assorted chips, sticks, etc. (it will just have to be thrown out otherwise)
8:37	Two seltzer tablets in glass of water

Total: just 719 calories!
A fraction of your usual dinner intake!

The Thin Food Diet

Calories are the most widely used measure of a given food's effect on your waistline, but common sense suggests that an equally reliable way of evaluating meals is by calculating their actual poundage. Until all the results are in, I recommend adopting a "weight-and-see" attitude.

Compare the two meals below. The first is composed entirely of "fat foods" that are thought of (goodness knows why) as being ideal for someone who is dieting.

Summer squash	2	pounds
Turnips (average serving)	½	
Head of cabbage	1½	
Lima beans	½	
Zucchini	4	
Tomatoes	1	(each)
Grapefruit	1½	
Total	14	pounds!

The alternative to giving your diet a heavyweight knockout punch is to plan to "eat light" at least once a week:

Thursday

Shrimp Cocktail	1½ ounces
Fettucine Alfredo	6
Filet of Sole Meunière	5
Whipped Potatoes	4
Napoleon Pastry	2½
Champagne (mostly bubbles anyway)	3
Total	Less than a pound and a half!

Honestly, which would you choose for your diet? The hefty
artichoke on the left or the light-as-a-feather pastry on the right?

The Little Bit of Everything Diet

From reading the preceding recipes, you have obviously discovered that I
normally eat very sparingly. Not only does this help me preserve my excep-
tional figure, but it also keeps me from feeling so full that I can't take teensy
tastes of my dining companions' meals. This way, I get to sample all of the

fare at a dinner instead of being limited to the one thing I have ordered and wishing I had had something else instead. Here is a representative evening out with a dear friend:

Friday

Grapefruit Juice
(*A smidgen of Kermie's Onion Rings*)
Tunafish Salad
(*Just a morsel or two of Kermie's Hamburger*)
Sliced Tomatoes
(*A few little nibbles at Kermie's French Fries*)
Fresh Fruit
(*A couple of tiny bites from Kermie's Peach Pie*)
Iced Tea
(*A dainty swallow of Kermie's Milkshake*)

The Saturday Splurge

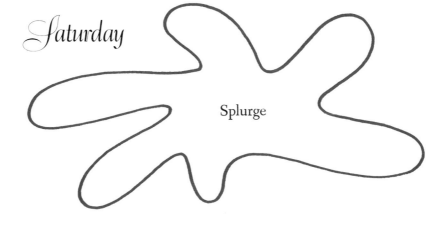

Saturday

Splurge

Some Final Diet Tips

1. Do not weigh yourself constantly. Every time you stand on the scales, it stretches the little springs and wing nuts inside and slowly presses them flat—the result, *even with no weight gain whatsoever,* is that the scale makes you appear to weigh a little more each time.

2. There is no such thing as a "correct" weight for any particular height—there are only averages. And moi, who has a perfect figure, can tell you that the idea of going on a diet is *not* to become so thin that when you are at a party and turn sideways, people think you left early.

3. If you do not like it, do not eat it. No matter how good it is supposed to be for you, it is just taking up space for something you do like. You can eliminate a lot of calories on the very first day of your diet by entirely cutting out things you hate.

4. Never eat anything at one sitting that you can't lift.

5. Always use one of the new—and far more reliable—elastic measuring tapes to check on your waistline.

BEFORE   AFTER

If you desire a slimmeur you, all you have to do is follow moi's advice, and voila!, les pounds simply melt away.

Entertaining

I have always thought that it is very important to be entertaining, and I work ultra-hard to be the best possible guest. You should, too. I must tell you, cher purchaseur de this book, it always amazes moi how many people know where to put the forks, what wine goes with succotash, and the best way to make beets look and taste like something else, but do not have the slightest idea how to make someone else's party a real success. I receive many invitations to all sorts of parties, and I accept them as often as I can, because I know that it is practically impossible these days for hosts to find persons to invite who really appreciate the fine points of party attendance.

How to Be the Perfect Guest

As with so much else in life, when it comes to guestology, planning is the quiche to success. You simply cannot take anything for granted, and that includes getting an invitation to a party in the first place.

You see, moi is *constantly* sought after for soirées, moirés, openings, closings, and other fancy occasions, but *vous*, who may just be starting out on your way to le top, should not sit back and wait for an invitation. If you do, all sorts of unfortunate mishaps may occur, and the only invitations you'll ever receive will be to join the Soup of the Month Club or buy a bunch of teensy medallions commemorating the Pets of the Vice Presidents. So many things can go wrong. An incorrect zip code could speed your invitation to some state you can't even spell. A meteorite might demolish your mailbox. Spontaneous combustion in the postman's mailbag could scorch your invitation so badly that the address is unreadable.

For this reason, whenever you hear about a party you would like to go to, you should make a point of letting the host know right away that you will be able to attend. People planning parties always appreciate your thoughtfulness in contacting them as early as possible.

The Early Bird Gets the Worm—Which Is What He Deserves

I am sure that you have heard the expression "fashionably late." Why is it fashionable to be late? Because if you have gone to a great deal of trouble with your outfit, you certainly do not want to play to an "empty house" when you make your entrance. Equally important: before actually entering, peek through the windows and try to get a feel for where the best lighting is. You may even decide to slip in the back way, creep up the kitchen stairs, and then slowly descend the main staircase.

After acknowledging applause with a smile and a teensy bow, step forward and give your host and the other guests an opportunity to greet you.

There are four basic ways of responding to this courtesy:

Complete Stranger

Acquaintance

Dear Friend

Kermit!

Some Straight Talk About Gifts

A fairly common social gaffe committed by well-meaning people is to call up on the day of the party to inquire if there is anything they can bring. Never do this. It suggests that you think your hosts are not capable of shopping for themselves or are the sort of people who are so hopelessly absent-minded that they are even likely to have forgotten something important, like dessert.

Obviously, the same rule holds true for bringing a small "house gift." Although your hosts will undoubtedly be too polite to do anything but accept it graciously, they will be secretly mortified. And if your gift is particularly lavish, it can prove terribly awkward, because they may mistake you for one of the delivery men and tip you.

On the other hand, it is perfectly all right for your hosts to offer *you* a small gift. (I encourage this increasingly widespread custom.) It shows in a very nice way how much they appreciate your taking time away from a busy schedule to come to their social gathering. If their gift is something especially nice, which you might like to give one of to a friend sometime, it is perfectly proper to inquire where it was purchased and how much it cost.

Similarly, if at some point in the evening you spot some little thing of your hosts that you would really enjoy having, it is quite acceptable for you to say something like, "Oh, what a nice little bowl—I would certainly like to have one just like it, but I cannot imagine how I would ever obtain one, EXCEPT PERHAPS AS A GIFT." This direct approach eliminates an awful lot of beating around the bush and gives your hosts such a graceful way to show how much they have enjoyed your company.

The Perfect Setting

Once the greetings are over, your host will take your things and go to fetch your refreshment. This is a perfect time to stroll over to the dining table and give the seating arrangements a once-over. Remember: it just is not fair to expect people to read your mind about your preferences for dining companions. Of course, they will always do the best they can, but it really is up to you to make your wishes known.

I have also found that on the whole, place cards are a bit drab and hard to read, and I like to be sure that my place is marked appropriately. This little photo shows you the sort of thing I mean.

Good hosts understand that certain guests—like moi—deserve a more lavish billing.

Once you have determined where you will be sitting, find some subtle way to get your hosts out of the room (I usually sniff loudly and say, "Hmmm, that smells like smoldering insulation. Do you suppose that you have an undiscovered electrical fire in the basement?"), and then rearrange the place cards to your liking.

Breaking the Ice

While you and your hosts are waiting for latecomers to arrive, it is up to you to make conversation. Remember, your hosts don't want to talk about their interests, or their house, or their hobbies and occupations. They already know all about those. What they want to hear about is *you*. Their anecdotes and jokes are pretty familiar to them by now; *yours* are fresh.

However, it is perfectly appropriate for you to be curious about your hosts and to take steps to satisfy that curiosity. By far the best way to do

Hmmmm, let's see, allergy pills, ear drops, contact-lens cleaner
—oooooh, there is plenty of good conversational material in *here!*

this is not by trying to "draw them out," but by taking advantage of the earliest opportunity to go up to their bathroom and examine the contents of their medicine chest.

Then when you enter into a conversation with them, they will be amazed and pleased at your informed interest in the teensy details of their daily lives. "That hair dye seems to be working wonders, Mr. So-and-so," you might observe, or, "Tell moi, Mrs. Such-and-such, do you find that the new denture creams are more effective than the old powders?"

If for any reason the conversation seems to lag a little, you can introduce your hosts to your clothes. "This is my latest hat," you could say. "It is from Paris." Or, "I would so much like you to meet my shoes—they are very stylish, as you can see, and they only cost twenty dollars."

If you see a few people who really don't seem to be getting into the swing of things, it is going to be up to you to get them involved. I find that a good way to do this is to get two or three people who are sort of hanging

This is not a particularly complicated game, but good bottle control
is absolutely essential.

back, maneuver them together, and then say something thought-provoking
like, "I think the center of the earth is filled with mayonnaise—what do *you*
think?" Once things get going, I slip away and tackle the next bunch of
wall flour.

    If the guests just will *not* mix, you may as a last resort want to propose
a party game. The one illustrated here—spin-the-bottle—is quite effective.

The Guestest with the Bestest

When dinner time comes, do not make the mistake of trying to "help" your
hosts with the serving. You will only spoil their split-second timing. And
anyway, you are not a serving person—you are the guest. It is your job to
be looked at, listened to, fed, and thanked.

During dinner, if you find that some part of the meal really has not worked out well at all, don't be afraid to send it back. The best way for your hosts to improve their cooking is to be told honestly about any shortcomings.

Never be shy about asking for seconds, and if there is only one of something on a plate, don't be bashful about taking it. Your hosts knew how many people were coming and will certainly have provided for their needs.

Some hosts are a little tongue-tied when it comes to proposing toasts to their guests, so I usually bring along a little note for whomever is seated at the head of the table. On it are a few words of appreciation for my helpfulness and just a word or two mentioning my most recent accomplishments.

When you leave, make sure you give your host and hostess an opportunity to thank you for coming. They will feel badly about not having had a chance to express to you personally their gratitude for your guest-pitality.

I often send a "bread-and-butter" report—just a few short words complimenting my hosts on successful aspects of the evening and tactfully pointing out areas that could stand improvement. Here is a sample:

Dear ____,

    I could see how happy you were to have me at your dinner, and I just wanted to write to tell you that I enjoyed myself very much. The hors d'oeuvres were on the whole excellent, with the exception of the sour cream dip which was a little tasteless. Dinner was delicious! The hollandaise sauce was particularly good. One little thing I would really look out for in the future, though, is overcooking the broccoli—it was ever so slightly mushy.

    I thought your choice of guests was for the most part very well made. I must say, however, that I wonder about Dr. ____, who took a rather offhand observation I made about comets being filled with marmalade in entirely the wrong way. He may be deranged.

    Your toast was so touching. I know you can't thank me enough for attending your party, but it was sweet of you to try!

        Yours,

        Miss Piggy
        xx

Exercise

I cannot tell you how many times people have come up to me to compliment me on my lavish figure. And always these dear, sweet people are dying to know what exercise program I use to maintain my ravishing bodée. I tell them what I will tell you: the object of exercise is to achieve your beauty aspirations without perspiration.

The Bedroom — Your Own Private Gymsnoozium

Anyone who has seen those speeded-up films they have made of persons sleeping knows that the average individual probably gets more exercise asleep than anywhere else. But you must not be so exhausted from unnecessary physical activity during the day itself that you just lie there, too sore to take full advantage of your "beauty wrestle."

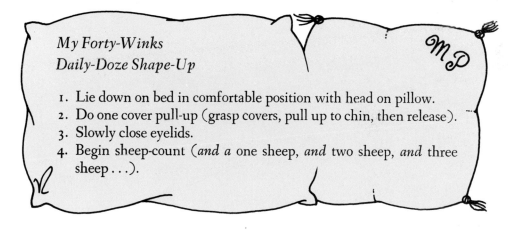

My Forty-Winks
Daily-Doze Shape-Up

1. Lie down on bed in comfortable position with head on pillow.
2. Do one cover pull-up (grasp covers, pull up to chin, then release).
3. Slowly close eyelids.
4. Begin sheep-count (*and a* one sheep, *and* two sheep, *and* three sheep . . .).

Are Your Clothes Fit?

If your wardrobe is not getting enough exercise, it can quickly get "out of shape." I strongly recommend taking a few minutes each day to give your garments a good stretching with some "loosening-up" exercises. All this

The Importance of Exercising Your Clothing. As you can see, this cute frock has a very bad case of closet cramps—it has lost its "bustle tone" and is much too far gone to whip back into shape. This sort of thing can be avoided with a regular wardrobe workout.

involves is trying on everything in your closet. (A word to the wise: if you find that one or more of your garments need replacing, do not automatically purchase another of the same size. I am very sorry to say that the inflation we are now experiencing applies to sizes as well as prices, and you will find that a given measurement—say 26—is really only last year's 23 or 24 and simply will not fit. I am afraid this is something we are going to have to adjust to.)

Exercising Caution

Many people embark impulsively on an ill-considered program of planned physical activity without giving any thought to the often very strenuous exercises they are already doing. If you are like moiself, you are leading such an active life that additional exertion is both pointless and foolhardy. The few examples below give an excellent picture of my exhausting physical program, and explain why, when it comes to additional exercise, I do a "Daily Doesn't."

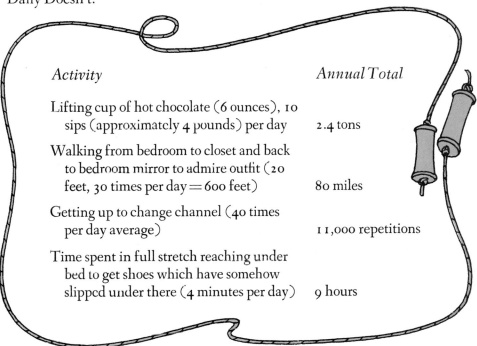

Activity	*Annual Total*
Lifting cup of hot chocolate (6 ounces), 10 sips (approximately 4 pounds) per day	2.4 tons
Walking from bedroom to closet and back to bedroom mirror to admire outfit (20 feet, 30 times per day = 600 feet)	80 miles
Getting up to change channel (40 times per day average)	11,000 repetitions
Time spent in full stretch reaching under bed to get shoes which have somehow slipped under there (4 minutes per day)	9 hours

Don't Throw a Physical Fit

You may already be fit *and not even know it*. Take this teensy test and see. Give yourself one point for each "yes" answer. If you score more than 5, you should stick to a lo-calisthenic diet.

1. Are you able to take elevators without getting winded?
2. Do you run to the phone at least three times a week?
3. Can you walk five blocks with a broken heel?
4. From a standing position, can you get 50 cents in change out of your purse without setting it down?

5. Can you make and eat a cake in under one hour?
6. With your hands at your sides, can you swing your hair in a complete circle with a single motion of your head?

Channel Your Energies

Every young lady should include a regular sports program in her schedule. In most areas, one or more television stations offer a good selection of such programs to choose from. However, before beginning to watch any strenuous athletic activity, I recommend "warming up" with a cup of cocoa, and if you notice any of the symptoms of overexertion listed below, take a breather.

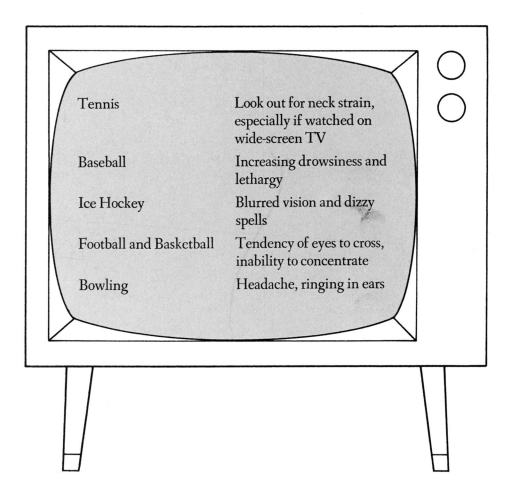

Tennis	Look out for neck strain, especially if watched on wide-screen TV
Baseball	Increasing drowsiness and lethargy
Ice Hockey	Blurred vision and dizzy spells
Football and Basketball	Tendency of eyes to cross, inability to concentrate
Bowling	Headache, ringing in ears

When one is as busy with a career as moi, one has to rely on
professionals to handle the more time-consuming aspects of one's
exercise program. I have a very nice man who operates this lovely
machinery for me (he *does* let the things get a little dusty), and there
is a perfectly charming young lady who comes in twice a week to do
yoga for me. They are such a help.

Fun Can Be Exercise

Your hobbies and recreational pursuits are an important source of exercise. I have a number of personal favorites. For example, I find that a vigorous round of shopping (at least one store an hour) is both stimulating and refreshing. (A word of warning: if you are a little out of condition, I would begin with some light window shopping, and build up gradually from there.) At first, try on just a few small things, like shoes, hats, and gloves, and then move on to whole outfits and the heavier coats and furs. Within a very short time, you should have developed a really active charge account, and you will be ready to tackle advertised close-outs and storewide clearance sales.

Why Stars Like Moi Have Heavenly Bodies

Although climbing to the very tippée top of my profession is the exercise I find the most enjoyable and rewarding, I do have a very special series of movements which I perform regularly to maintain the full, womanly shape my Kermit likes. I have chosen a few to illustrate here to give you an idea of the immense amount of work that goes into being a superstar.

Basic Beauty-Building

Every day, I do a number of different pin-up exercises to enhance my perfect posture. These are basically four-count exercises, and you can do them at any speed you like. To get the maximum benefit, you must be able to see yourself clearly in at least one full-length mirror, and if you notice that you are starting to perspire, stop immediately.

Beginning Pin-Up

1. Assume Standard Demure Starting Position, hands at sides, feet a comfortable distance apart, body facing mirror. 2. Put hands on hips, tilt head slightly to one side. 3. Place one hand on hair at back of head and bend opposite knee a teensy bit. 4. Pivot on foot, shifting weight as you turn head and eyes up, and say, "Ooooooooooooooooh." (This position can be held as long as you like.)

1.

2.

3.

4.

Intermediate Pin-Up

1. Move toward cushion or divan in Basic Seat-Approach Pose, hands outstretched, legs bent slightly at knee. 2. Gently sit down and fold hands sweetly on lap. 3. Cross legs. 4. Place one hand on hip, other hand on hair, lean back, and smile. (Eyelash flutter should not be attempted until basic movement is mastered.)

1.

2.

3.

4.

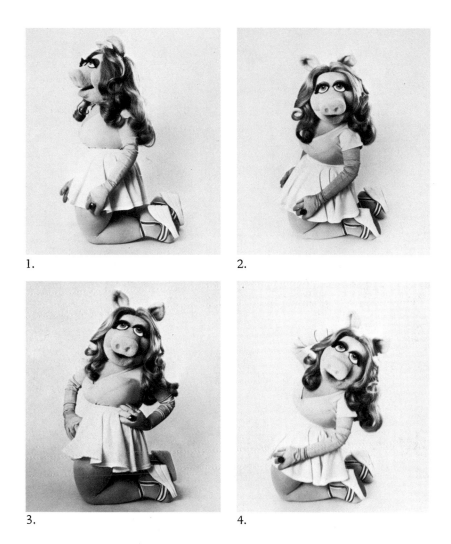

1.

2.

3.

4.

Advanced Pin-Up ("The Grable")

1. Place yourself in Semi-Lounge Position, knees on soft carpet, hands at sides with elbows bent, gaze directed upward. 2. Execute a half-turn and smile. 3. Place hand on hip and lean back slightly. 4. Move hand to hair and go into Deep Longing Gaze with Modified Coy Finish.

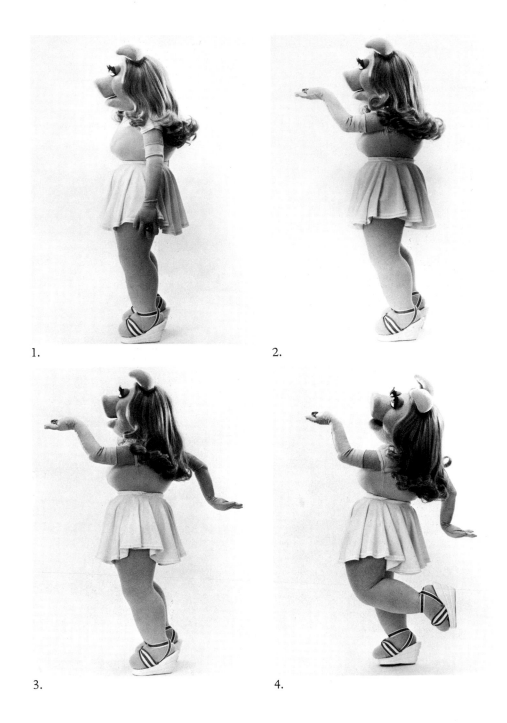

1.

2.

3.

4.

Optional Beginning Pin-Up ("The Full Tut")

1. Assume Demure Profile Position. 2. Raise left arm into half-Cleo.
3. Raise right arm into three-quarter Cleo. 4. Raise left leg and execute
full Vertical Eye-Roll with Single Hair Toss.

Niceometric Exercises

Powdering your nose is a stimulating physical action which most ladies do six or eight times a day, giving them an excellent opportunity to tone their physiques.

The Freshen-Up

1. Look in mirror with puff in hand. 2. Tilt head and s-l-o-w-l-y raise puff. 3. When puff is parallel to nose, hold in Pretouch Position for a few seconds. 4. Touch puff to nose lightly a few times with a full stretching movement of the arm on each application of powder. (Some women use special weighted puffs for extra exercise value, but I definitely do not recommend this.)

1.

2.

3.

4.

Another exercise which is a pleasure to do is telephoning a friend. I call Kermit—oh, I do not know, maybe two or three times a day, certainly no more than twenty—and this provides a pleasant way to "telephone-tone" my arms.

1.   2.   3.

The Call-Up

1. Sit comfortably in Predial Position. 2. Lift receiver and dial number (long-distance calls are more demanding—look out for finger strain). 3. Balance weight of receiver by placing other hand on table as you talk with your friend. If you notice any strain, shift receiver to other hand. (I improve my finger flexibility for this exercise by doing "gemnastics," a series of finger lifts accomplished while wearing a full complement of jewelry. This also strengthens my autograph-signing hand.)

Accepting large gifts has a very good effect both on your mood and your upper body. This is my favorite exercise.

The Gift Lift ✒

1. Seat yourself comfortably with hands folded in "Surely Nothing Wonderful Is Going to Happen in the Next Five Minutes" Position. 2. Lean back, place one hand on chest, other on hair, in "Perhaps There Has Been Some Mistake" Pose. 3. Extend hands and delicately snatch gift. 4. Hold gift on lap in firm, two-handed grasp (if your grip is correct, gift cannot be removed without heavy equipment).

1.

2.

3.

4.

A morning cup of tea or hot chocolate is as invigorating an exercise as it is a beverage.

The Sip-Up

1. Sit at breakfast table with cup in easy reach. 2. Place fingers on cup handle and prepare to lift. (Remember: keep back straight and don't lean into the cup, otherwise you may develop "teaneck.") 3. Raise cup to lips and take teensy sips, then return to saucer. (A little note: in international "Gold Cup" competition, points are subtracted for spills, slurps, and any audible china noises.)

1.   2.   3.

When You Are Hot, You Turn on the Fans

Like any superstar, I have a public figure, and I must be prepared at all times for the rigors of life lived in the limelight. I know that when I am recognized by crowds of adoring fans (this can happen dozens of times in a single day), I have an obligation to return their wild enthusiasm with appropriate—and physically demanding—gestures. And this means being in absolutely top physical condition at all times.

Admirer Greeting (Simplified)

1. This is the right position in which to prepare to acknowledge praise and adoration. Note that my weight is evenly distributed, and I can simply turn and execute a Profile Hair-Twirl without any awkwardness if, due to conditions of unusually poor visibility, I am not recognized. 2. As the crowd applauds and cheers, I am going to want to move into a medium "Who, Moi?" Being able to hold this pose long enough to create the desired effect takes training. 3. A slight bending of the knees, a quarter-turn, and a Two-handed Hair-Preen converts the previous position into a classic "Refusal to Believe That Such Fuss Is Warranted Pirouette." 4. You need stamina to be able to follow up these three positions with a full "Acknowledgment of Widespread Infatuation" but that is what moi's public expects and deserves.

1.

2.

turnez le page ☞

3.   4.

To greet a dear friend who is at some distance, a more personal gesture is called for, for instance:

The Cross-Town Buss 🪶

1. Adopt Presmooch Pose. 2. Take a deep breath and raise hand to mouth. 3. Propel kiss outward with a smooth sweep of the hand, exhale, and then politely shout "Kissy-kissy!"

(A modest variation of this exercise is very handy for hailing a cab.)

1.

2.

3.

It is an unfortunate fact that some people make such nuisances of themselves that they must be thoroughly discouraged whenever they appear. For such individuals, a cold shoulder is the perfect demonstration of distaste, but be careful. Unless you have put in the many hours of practice I have, you can severely pull a muscle or even suffer a dislocation.

The Short Rebuff (three basic phases)

1. The neutral or passive phase. 2. A smooth transition to Total Nose-down Disdain. 3. The Full-twist Snub with Hand on Hip and High-angle Disgusted Gaze (there just isn't space here for the highly effective, but far more elaborate, 16-part Complete Rebuff).

1.

2.

3.

My Stocking Run

I really do not understand why a lady would run if nothing is chasing her, but jogging clothes are quite cute, and the Key Track Positions are ideal for modeling them. (Of course, if you actually *are* a joggeur—and many, many of my friends are—I recommend that you do your running in old clothes. You will be going much too fast for anyone to have a proper chance to appreciate your outfit—top designers call this problem "fashion blur"—and you are likely to get road goo or track fuzz or whatever it is all over those very stylish shoes.)

1.

2.

3.

4.

5.

Racing in Place

1. On your mark. 2. Get ready. 3. Get set. 4. Go. 5. Winning the race. (For Receiving First Prize, see p. 56, The Gift Lift.)

Fashion

If you wish to be truly chic—and who in her right mind does not—you must be willing to say Phooez! to fads. Classic fashion is forever.

By classic fashion, I mean those styles which, because of their elegantude, have survived the test of time. Remember, what is the rage today is a rag tomorrow. Shoes that should be worn by shot-putters, earrings the size of belt buckles, belt buckles the size of earrings—I have seen them all come and go.

Take it from moi, the only way to have high-fashion impact is to refuse to go along with flash-in-le-pan apparel trends. When a lady in a well-cut suit with a pretty chapeau walks down a street filled with people with wheels on their shoes and paint in their hair, she immediately becomes the fashion focus.

I know this because I am a pig, and as a pig, I have always stood out. Yes, it takes courage to be different, and there have been those who have made fun of moi, but consider: it is moi's book you are reading, not theirs. Enough. Let us examine the Fashion Fundamentals.

Les Basiques	Les Optionals	Les Boo-Boos
Silk	Taffeta	Polyester
Satin	Ruffles	Ultrasuede
Lamé	Sequins	Doubleknits
Cashmere	Frills	Madras
Mohair	Crêpe	Mesh
Chocolate	Chenille	Wooden jewelry
One large jewel	Chiffon	Anything tie-dyed
Lavender gloves	Mocha	Holes
Heels and pearls	Fleece	Spots
Lip gloss	Doodads (if tasteful)	Lint

A Closet Odyssey

Let us take a petit tour of moi's closette. I find that it is very handy to arrange things by colors. I have a drawer here filled with purple things, one for blue, a very large one for green, and so on. I suppose you could do it alphabetically but you would waste so much time trying to decide if shirts come before skirts and whether a loden-green Harris tweed polo coat should go under "L," "G," "H," "T," "P," or "C."

By the way, I don't use those awful wire hangers the dry cleaners send your clothes back on and neither should you. I use hangers padded with dark red velvet. They are au courant for the closette. As a matter of fact, it is far better to allow your clothes to recline comfortably on a chair, the bed, or even the floor than to subject them to the stresses and strains of improper hanging.

Gowns. You cannot have too many gowns, any more than you can have too many invitations to parties to wear them to. The two go hand in hand. People don't just invite *you*—they invite your clothes as well. (Sometimes when I can't attend a party I particularly want to go to, I will send a teensy note describing what I would have worn.)

Hats are a wonderful part of any lady's wardrobe. They are so pretty and add such a lot to any outfit. Not only that, but in a very undependable and often upsetting world, they are absolutely reliable—your hat size *never* changes. I don't keep my hats in any one place. I prefer to spread them around. They are like acquaintances, and it is always a pleasant surprise to encounter one I have not seen in a while in some unexpected place. For example, I might be doing a teensy bit of dusting somewhere—a sort of depressing chore—and voilà! I am reintroduced to that cute blue chapeau with the little bunch of flowers. So nice to see you again!

And last, but not le least, I have one whole shelf set aside just for handbags. I find that it is vital to have at least one handbag for each of the ten types of social occasion: Very Formal, Not So Formal, Just a Teensy Bit Formal, Informal But Not *That* Informal, Every Day, Every Other Day, Day Travel, Night Travel, Theater, and Fling. Transferring essentials from one to another is a time-consuming process, so keep them all fully stocked with the Basic Purse Load: hankies, keys, change, little mints, makeup, hairpins, lemon drops, nail file, bonbons, extra gloves, ribbon, hard candy in cellophane, a notepad, pastilles, perfume, butterscotch, a pen, toffee, chocolate kisses, a mirror, and, of course, fudge.

One's chapeau provides the perfect opportunity for a profound fashion statement. Your hat should not merely say, "here is my head," but rather it should convey a sense of allure, mystery, even intrigue. Here moi's chapeau is saying, "Oui, I have time for one quick chocolate malted in that cafe with the umbrellas that have tables on their handles, but then I must board the Oriental Express for a rendezvous with the Duke of Candelabra in the lovely, yet sinister, Kingdom of Rutabagia."

The Nittez-Grittez—Duds That Are Duds

The following clothing is *always* out of style as far as moi is concerned:

Metallic Jackets: If you are not planning to travel at the speed of smell in the near future, I cannot imagine why you would want to wear anything made out of the stuff they build airplane fuselages out of.

Enormous Quilted Down-Filled Jackets: These are bulky and have no style whatsoever. They make you look as if you have taken the part of the big pineapple in the Pageant of Tropical Fruits.

Sack Dresses and Caftans: These are nothing but shapeless bags. The feminine figure is not meant to be hidden with dust covers like the furniture in a closed-up summer house.

Skirts with Huge Safety Pins: Oh, I hate those horrid pins. Give them to the zoo for elephant diapers.

Leg Warmers: Yuque! Ptuez! Ooooooooh, le worst!

Good "Looks" You Didn't Have to Be Born With

It is much easier than you would think to cut the sort of figure you have always dreamed of.

For the "thin" look: Buy clothes two sizes too large.

For the "rich" look: Leave a couple of price tags on "accidentally," and add zeros where they will do the most good.

For the "important" look: Wear your coat loosely around your shoulders like a cape, with your arms outside the sleeves; wear dark glasses; and from time to time reach into your purse and talk on the telephone which you have placed there.

For the "glamorous" look: Choose plain-looking dining companions.

The Finishing Touch—How Much?

A well-known architect named someone or other once said, "Less is more." That is the silliest thing I have ever heard. Less is *less*. Unfortunately, a good deal of what passes for modern fashion has been influenced by the regrettable trend toward understatement. How many times I have observed otherwise stylishly attired ladies in outfits that simply failed to catch fire because they neglected to add those few itsée-bitsée details that add focus to a costume, details like a good-sized flower (depending on the season, a rhododendron bloom, a hyacinth, or a large lily), a dramatic silk sash, a fancy hair comb, a sizable brooch that lights up, a feathered boa, a Belgian lace shawl, a mantilla, a tiara, a fichu—whatever strikes your fancy! Before you go out on that important date, conduct your own "dress rehearsal." Stand as far away from your mirror as you can and look at yourself through the wrong end of a pair of opera glasses. Do you stand out? Can they see you from the balcony? If not, you need to add some fashion flash. After all, what is the use of being a fashion plate if all you are going to put on it is peas?

Oui and Non

Fashion is not merely dressing well. The essence of fashion lies in choice, in knowing the good from the bad, gold from mere dross, in all the many aspects of your life. Unless you have that rare mixture of taste and experience which moi has, you cannot, of course, be expected to know instantly whether something is Right. But perhaps this teensy list will help you develop your own fashion sense.

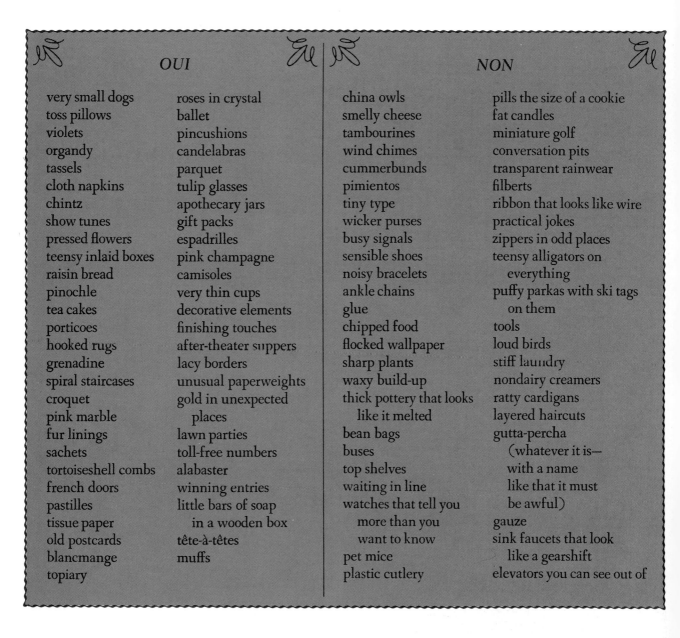

OUI

very small dogs	roses in crystal
toss pillows	ballet
violets	pincushions
organdy	candelabras
tassels	parquet
cloth napkins	tulip glasses
chintz	apothecary jars
show tunes	gift packs
pressed flowers	espadrilles
teensy inlaid boxes	pink champagne
raisin bread	camisoles
pinochle	very thin cups
tea cakes	decorative elements
porticoes	finishing touches
hooked rugs	after-theater suppers
grenadine	lacy borders
spiral staircases	unusual paperweights
croquet	gold in unexpected
pink marble	places
fur linings	lawn parties
sachets	toll-free numbers
tortoiseshell combs	alabaster
french doors	winning entries
pastilles	little bars of soap
tissue paper	in a wooden box
old postcards	tête-à-têtes
blancmange	muffs
topiary	

NON

china owls	pills the size of a cookie
smelly cheese	fat candles
tambourines	miniature golf
wind chimes	conversation pits
cummerbunds	transparent rainwear
pimientos	filberts
tiny type	ribbon that looks like wire
wicker purses	practical jokes
busy signals	zippers in odd places
sensible shoes	teensy alligators on
noisy bracelets	everything
ankle chains	puffy parkas with ski tags
glue	on them
chipped food	tools
flocked wallpaper	loud birds
sharp plants	stiff laundry
waxy build-up	nondairy creamers
thick pottery that looks	ratty cardigans
like it melted	layered haircuts
bean bags	gutta-percha
buses	(whatever it is—
top shelves	with a name
waiting in line	like that it must
watches that tell you	be awful)
more than you	gauze
want to know	sink faucets that look
pet mice	like a gearshift
plastic cutlery	elevators you can see out of

Here moi is demonstrating the two basic categories of high fashion: le day outfit (above) and le night outfit (left). The daytime, with its pale, poorly focused natural light, calls for a fairly forthright fashion statement. On the other hand, during the evening hours, when more professional illumination is available, your goal should be an understated—yet audible—elegance.

HOW TO AVOID WEIGHT LOSS
IN THE COMING LEAN YEARS

Finance

Fortunately, I have always had very sound business sense, and so keeping my affairs in order has never presented much of a problem for moi.

Business sense isn't being able to predict the price of peppermint, or knowing when to get out of tea cozies and into doilies and little dishes, or being able to tell in advance that there is going to be a glut of maraschino cherries in Umbrellastan. And by business sense, I certainly do not mean being able to add up a column of figures as long as a stepladder and come up with the same dull total time after time. There are inexpensive little machines the size of a box of cough drops that do that quite satisfactorily.

What I *am* talking about is that certain flair for dealing with complex money matters effortlessly and with style.

From Cash to Cashes

Many people think money is something to be set aside for a rainy day. But honestly, how much money do you really *need* for a dozen or so hours of inclement weather?

The fact of the matter is that just like almost everything else green (I specifically exclude emeralds and a certain very dear frog), money can get stale quite quickly. I know you wouldn't think of putting fresh asparagus in the back of a drawer and eating it three months later, and yet otherwise sensible people do take sizable amounts of money and pretty much let it rot.

You see, the longer money is held on to, the more likely it is to suffer from what is technically termed cashosis or decashification. But never mind the nomenclature. I know that you have seen the awful results. Two or three crackling clean ten-dollar bills folded neatly in a purse and left for a week or two turn into seven greasy ones and some nickels and pennies.

Large amounts of paper money are also a fire hazard, and the prudent individual sees to it that major accumulations are avoided. Although purse blazes are a relatively uncommon occurrence, there is just no reason to be smug or complacent about the potential threat.

Don't Bank on It

A lot of people will also urge you to put some money in a bank, and in fact—within reason—this is very good advice. But don't go overboard. Remember, what you are doing is giving your money to somebody else to hold on to, and I think that it is worth keeping in mind that the businessmen who run banks are so worried about holding on to things that they put little chains on all their pens.

It also is a simple fact that when you "save" money, all you are doing is lending it to someone else to spend. It seems to me that since you earned it, most of the time it ought to be you who does the spending.

Dollars and Sense

Choosing a bank is a fairly straightforward procedure. All banks are pretty much the same. There are two things to look for. First, inspect the window: if a bank doesn't look like a hardware store, pass it by. All of them give free gifts for opening an account, but none of them does it all the time, and the gifts vary considerably. Banks that do not have enough sense to offer really good gifts are certain to be poorly run.

The other important thing to investigate is a bank's selection of check designs and checkbook covers. Many banks offer very little to choose from in the way of check pictures—often just that same old shot of a sick-looking pine tree on the California coast or a lot of wet people on a sailboat. You are going to have to look at that scene every time you pay a bill, and it should be something that cheers you up.

You also want to make doubly sure that your checkbook is balanced— that is, that the colors of your checkbook, your checkbook cover, and your purse do not clash. A predominantly blue check design, with a brown cover, in a cream-colored purse would be just terrible.

Paying Your IOU's

Everyone has to pay tax. The way to look at it is this: each year you are buying a few things you didn't think you were buying, like a couple of shrubs for the White House, or a new desk for the Secretary of Big Boats.

They send you a bill for it due April 15, and if you are not prepared for it, that can ruin your fun, just when the weather is getting warm. (They never tell you *exactly* what it is you are spending the money for, which I think is both unfair and not very smart. After all, if they said that what they needed was twenty pairs of socks for the Marines, I know I could pick out something much nicer than what they are going to end up getting, or if what they wanted was some paint for a Post Office, I certainly wouldn't choose that vile yellow.)

You're Stuck If You Can't Budget

The essence of managing money is managing to have enough of it when you need it. This takes some careful planning.

1. Long-Range Expense Forecast

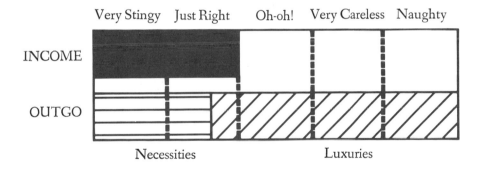

Note that necessities and luxuries are separated. It is up to each person to decide for herself which is which, but some things, like a bare minimum of ten dresses, a good color television set, and at least one movie a week, are clearly necessities, while excessive visits to the dentist, library memberships, and savings bonds are typical luxuries. As the chart shows, you have to know where to draw the line.

If you like, you can focus on certain specific areas in your financial picture to get a better idea of where your money is going. See Chart #2 on page 76.

2. CANDY BAR GRAPH (seasonally adjusted)*

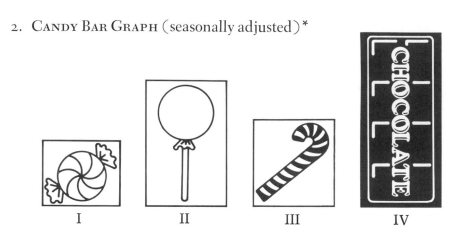

I   II   III   IV

*(Allowance for melting in Third Quarter)

It also helps to be able to plot graphically the daily ups and downs in your cash position. See Chart #3:

3. WEEKLY MONEY SUPPLY CHART

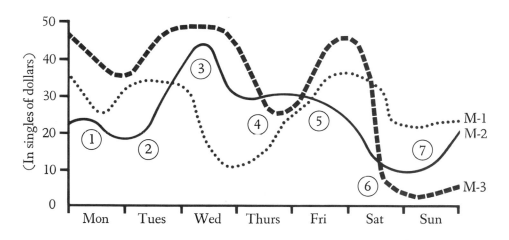

M-1: Money in purse   M-2: Money in purse plus money in top drawer under the hankies   M-3: M-1 + M-2 plus money in hatbox I can't find and loan to Gonzo.

1. Bought stockings; 2. found crumpled-up five in between sofa cushions; 3. check from my agent; 4. Kermit forgot his wallet on our date; 5. bought nice little brooch; 6. check from my agent bounces; 7. loan from Dancing Rats.

How to Avoid a Major Financial Depression

It can be very depressing to run low on money. Nevertheless, it is bound to happen to everyone sooner or later, and you should know how to handle it.

I do what big corporations do when they run into hard times: I put together a Report to the Stockholders (Me = 33⅓%; Myself = 33⅓%; and Moi = 33⅓%) which emphasizes the positive and plays down the bad news. Here is how one of my sample financial statements might read:

Assets		Liabilities	
Looks	$ 1,000,000.00	Owed to Dancing Rats	$10.00
Valued Friends	500,000.00 (A)	Outstanding Bills	74.26
Talent	750,000.00 (B)	TOTAL LIABILITIES	$84.26
Health	750,000.00		
Winning Personality	750,000.00		
Sense of Humor	1,000,000.00 (C)		
Brains	1,000,000.00		
Fans	100,000,000.00 (D)		
Cash on Hand	7.23		
Accounts Receivable	5.00 (E)		
TOTAL ASSETS	$104,525,512.23		

Notes:

A. A price can't be put on friendship. Listed amount indicates typical sum I would not trade my friends for.
B. Does not include hidden talents and unguessed-at abilities.
C. Priceless. Carried for accounting purposes at 1,000,000 laughs with a $1.00 par value each.
D. Conservative estimate.
E. From Kermit.

I have examined the preceding report and the accompanying Notes using my normal procedures, and in my opinion they present fairly and without qualification my true financial position.

Miss Piggy
xx

Food

Moi Cuisine

I just adore to cook, whether it is a little meal for moiself, a romantic supper for Kermit, or a dinner for a few dear friends. Unfortunately, I have so little time in my busy career that I must limit myself to just two basic kinds of cooking: very simple things that can be prepared with an absolute minimum of time and fuss, or much more elaborate recipes that can be cooked and served entirely by others and eaten in their homes (see "Entertaining").

In this chapter I have listed just a few of my most successful culinary presentations, but using my techniques you can come up with delightful, delectable, despeedy, and decheap meals of your own.

A Culinary "Flight of Fancy"

There is absolutely no reason why everyone can't enjoy airline cooking at home. It is not only a very convenient way to dine—for one thing, your kitchen doesn't have that awful "cooked-in" look when you're finished —but it also lends a welcome touch of adventure to even the most ordinary occasion. And since everything is designed to be served cold, it can be prepared days, even weeks, ahead of time.

Everything should be shiny and wrapped up in teensy packages, boxes, or cups, and served with plastic knives and forks and glasses on a foil tray. Little cheese and cracker packs, spreads that come in tubes, bags full of miniature candy bars, cups of coleslaw and potato salad from the deli, and jelly in those tiny plastic tubs are ideal plane food.

Just to add to the festive mood, before dinner I show everyone where all the exits are, and I put ribbons on the chairs for people to use as seat belts. When dinner is served, I turn on a vacuum cleaner in the bedroom for a little realistic engine noise, and every now and then I give the table a jolt with my knee and remark, "Don't worry, it is just light turbulence— we will be through it in a moment."

I also point out things in the room that guests sitting in various seats can see. "You folks on the right side of the table can get a nice view of the plants in the corner and my sofa," I might say, "and if you look down, you can see my new carpet."

When they get up to leave, I ask them to make sure they have all their personal belongings and give each one a complimentary plastic fork as a souvenir.

Dinner de Take-Out à la Belle Telephone

Smart chefs realize that the easiest cookbook to use is the Yellow Pages and the handiest appliance in the kitchen is the telephone. With it, you can turn out more delicious meals than with your oven, your broiler, your blender, and all your pots and pans combined. It's a pleasure to use—it is just about impossible to burn yourself on it or cut yourself with it—and best of all, when you're finished with it, it doesn't need to be washed. Moi, I prefer the push-button models, but the old-fashioned dial types, though a teensy bit slower and a trifle hard on the fingers, work just as well.

Here's a sample recipe:

Chinese Banquet

1. Dial 555-6780
2. Give order
3. No MSG, please!
4. Ask for extra fortune cookies
5. Give name and address
6. Get purse out

Note: The noodle dishes are terrible; no deliveries after 10 p.m.

Consult Mrs. Bell's wonderful "cookbook"...

Place your order...

When the doorbell rings, dinner is ready...

Take the food from the delivery man...

. . . and serve.

Of course, Chinese food is not the only cuisine you can "cook" with your telephone. And in fact, if I have guests over, I like to call several different places and put together a "Snacks de Many Nations" feast, with the different courses eaten in the order they arrive. It adds a nice bit of suspense to an already festive occasion as everyone tries to guess what's going to come through the door next!

Good-Looking Cooking

It is often said that cooking is an art, but I have had very few meals that I would hang on my wall. The truth is, food is awfully drab-looking most of the time. And the few foods that really are pretty, like turnips and beets and wax beans, taste as if you ate your purse by mistake.

But with a little bit of food coloring, you can transform even the most lackluster entrée into a feast for the eyes as well as the stomach. Scrambled eggs are so much more appealing when they are purple, and a commonplace spaghetti dinner becomes rare and exciting if you cook it in three different batches—say, orange, green, and pink—and then mix them all together.

And just imagine the cries of pleasure and surprise you will hear when you serve your guests lavender french fries, a plaid hamburger, and a blue milkshake! (A word of warning: gray or black food makes people nervous.)

How to Make Food French

One of the easiest ways to spice up a simple meal is to make it French. All you need is a pair of pinking shears, lots of those little ruffled paper hats they put on lamb chops, and a serving plate with a big round cover that has a handle on it. Use the shears to cut around the outside of anything fairly thin and hard, like slices of cucumber or cheese or bread, to give them that nice serrated edge. Put a little ruffle on anything long and thin, like celery or french fries or carrot sticks.

When you serve your guests, take everything to the table in the big dish, then lift off the cover with a dramatic flourish and say, for example, "Sandwich de Butter de Peanut avec Jellée sur bed of Potatoes Chippée, and on la side, les Pickles avec Little Hats on Them." Instantly, your dining companions are magically transported to a glamorous Parisian café, and even the most familiar fare is given a distinct foreign flavor.

Here is another little touch. Serve bottles of soft drinks wrapped in napkins in a bucket full of ice. Pour a little into your own glass, slosh it around, take a taste, and say, "Hmmm, a very nice grapefruit soda, with plenty of body and a good bouquet—it will develop a little more roundness if left in the refrigerator for another day or two, but frankly I think it's ready to drink right now," then fill your guests' glasses.

Bon appétit!

Manners

The Polite Touch — Your Ettiquestions Answered

I am sorry to say that very few people these days pay much attention to old-fashioned manners. I, of course, am an exception. To moi, beauty and good breeding are, like a pig and her frog, inseparable.

Still, I do realize that many personnes would like to behave properly, but simply do not know the correct thing to do in a given social situation.

Let us go over a few of the areas where common mistakes occur.

In the Restaurant

Some foods present particular problems for personnes who insist, as moi does, on proper table manners. The most troublesome:

Artichokes. These things are just plain annoying. Picking them apart to get at the good stuff is like trying to get the cashews out of a bowl of mixed nuts without getting stuck with one of those big hard white ones, and after all the trouble you go to, you get about as much actual "food" out of eating an artichoke as you would from licking thirty or forty postage stamps. Have the shrimp cocktail instead.

Chinese Food. You do not sew with a fork, and I see no reason why you should eat with knitting needles.

Clams. I simply cannot imagine why anyone would eat something slimy served in an ashtray.

French Fries. These may be taken, three or four at a time, from a dining companion's plate, with the fingers.

Fruits. A bowl of fruit is sometimes served in place of dessert. This practice should be discouraged. Slip these "purse foods" daintily into your handbag for a snack later, and demand that the pastry wagon be brought over, pronteau.

Lobsters. Although these are delicious, getting them out of their shells involves giving them quite a brutal going-over. The way I look at it, they never did anything to me (although they are quite nasty-looking, and I do not like the way they stare at you from those fish tanks when you come into the restaurant—it is quite rude). On the other hand, if they serve you just the good parts already removed from the shell, that is quite a different matter, since the element of personal participation in the massacre is eliminated.

Snails. I find this a somewhat disturbing dish, but the sauce is divine. What I do is order escargots, and tell them to "hold" the snails.

During dinner, it may be necessary to excuse yourself for a telephone call. However, it is far preferable to have a phone brought to the table, and the better restaurants have facilities for this. As a general rule, white telephones go with fish and poultry, and black ones with anything else. If you are calling during dessert, a small after-dinner phone should be used. The proper procedure is for the waiter bringing the phone to let you test it with a short call to a local number, and if the connection is bad or the telephone is in poor condition, it is quite all right to send it back. On the other hand, if you are satisfied, say something like, "Yes, it is a very nice, light telephone, with a good, clear tone and a smooth, almost velvety, dialing action."

There are several ways of calculating the tip after a meal. I find that the best is to divide the bill by the height of the waiter. Thus, a bill of $12.00 brought by a six-foot waiter calls for a $2.00 tip.

Weddings

Weddings are wonderful, but I do think they are a trifle dull for people who are not getting married. Kermie and I both agree that right now is not the proper time for our matrimonial nuptualities—my career, you see (the dear understands *completely*). But when the time comes, we intend to dispense with all the fuss and bother, and have a simple ceremony in a charming little country church, limited to just a dozen or so intimate friends—certainly no more than 500 at the absolute tops—and just a couple of pool reporters and one teensy camera crew.

Birthdays

The celebration of une's birthday is too critical a matter to be left to chance. Long in advance of the date, you should take advantage of the opportunity presented by visits to friends' homes to unobtrusively circle the date on their calendars and write a teensy reminder. Whenever making appointments or

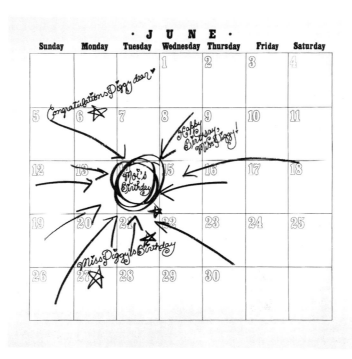

dates, always use your birthday as a convenient benchmark. "I will see you for lunch on the twenty-third," you might remark, casually adding, "which, as you may recall, is only forty-four days before my birthday." A week before your birthday, a formal announcement should be sent.

Miss Piggy is pleased to announce that she will be
celebrating her birthday this year on

Tuesday

RSVP (Runnez out and Shop for Votre Presents)

Thank-You Notes

Whenever you receive a gift, you must acknowledge it with a note expressing your thanks. The correct protocol, which I endorse, is to be as generous with your merci as they were with their gifts:

Teensy Gift	Thank you *or* Thanks so much.
Medium Gift	Thank you very much for the nice gift.
Largish Gift	Oh, thank you *so* much for giving me such a nice gift!
Gigantic Gift	Oh, thank you so very, very much for giving me such a wonderful, sweet gift! It was so truly thoughtful of you and I did so enjoy receiving it! You are an absolute dear.

Sticky Situations

Every day people find themselves in circumstances which call for the utmost in delicacy and diplomacy. Here are just a few of the most common, with my foolproof suggestions for how to handle them.

A good friend has appeared in an awful play, and you are at a loss to find something nice to say about it.

"I cannot tell you how comfortable our seats were—it was just like sitting in an easy chair at home!"

Someone you like is wearing an ugly hat, and she asks you to give her your honest opinion of it.

"What a lovely chapeau! But if I might make one teensy suggestion? If it blows off, don't chase it."

You accidentally knock over and break a vase in someone's house.

"Oh, thank goodness it was moi, and not some unscrupulous rascal who would have sued you for negligée in leaving this object in a dangerous location!"

Deck 'Em or Decorum?

Another kind of awkward moment is one in which you are confronted with really rotten behavior and have to choose between turning the other cheek and responding in a cool but civil manner or deciding that what is right is a good left. Test your *chemin de fer* with moi's P's and Q's I.Q. Quiz.

1. At a party, someone makes a play for your frog. You—
   a. Inform her politely that he is "spoken for."
   b. Give her a taste of handburger.

2. A passerby on the street makes a vulgar comment. You—
   a. Ignore him entirely.
   b. Make him a knuckle sandwich.

3. A person bumps into you on the street, knocking packages out of your hand, and neither apologizes nor offers to help pick them up. You—
   a. Tell him his discourtesy identifies him as a scoundrel.
   b. Let him chow down on a mitt blintz.

4. Someone cuts ahead of you in line. You—
   a. Inform him in a voice loud enough for others in line to hear that he is breaking in, and then direct him to the end of the line.
   b. Serve him a slice of palm quiche.

Answers: 1, b; 2, b; 3, b; 4, b.

Romance

What is love?

Love is the most wonderful thing in the world. When you are in love with someone, you want to be near him all the time, except when you are out buying things and charging them to him.

Is it all right to kiss on the first date?

It depends on how you feel about him. Here is my little rule, from the days before I met my Kermie: if he picks up the check, give him a peck; if it was dutch, no such luck.

What do you do if a man you like, and who likes you, still wants to see other women?

Although this is by definition a somewhat emotional matter, you should approach it in a calm, reasonable, mature way. What I would do is calmly, reasonably, and maturely explain to him that if he values his life, he should change his behavior.

What should a woman do if a man stands her up on a date?

If the man is genuinely apologetic, I would let him off with a large bunch of flowers, an expensive present, and a lavish makeup dinner. On the other hand, if he treats it in an offhand manner, he is obviously the kind of person who is not going to knock himself out for you, and you should do it for him.

If an engagement is broken, should the girl return gifts given to her by the boy?

This depends entirely on the circumstances. If the engagement was broken by mutual consent, I would say no. If the boy broke the engagement, then he certainly should not expect to get the presents back. If the girl feels that she must break the engagement, then I think it is really best that she keep the presents, since if they are returned, they will only serve as an unhappy reminder to him of the broken engagement.

Is there such a thing as love at first sight?

Definitely. The first time I met Kermie, I heard violins, I saw fireworks, and I felt as if I were walking on air. And Kermie says the first moment he saw me, his flippers tingled. At the time he thought that that meant it was going to rain, but later he realized its true meaning.

How can a girl control jealousy?

Any sensible girl knows that even if her boyfriend is madly in love with her, he is not going to stop looking at other women—it is just human nature. But she also knows that she can trust him, because she can tell in her heart that he is faithful, honest, and true, and because she never lets him out of her sight.

Is there a "cure" for a broken heart?

Only time can heal your broken heart, just as only time can heal his broken arms and legs.

How can you hint to someone you like very much that he has a habit you cannot stand, like chewing gum or cracking his knuckles?

Be honest. Two people who are really in love are always willing to make teensy changes in their habits to make life more pleasant for each other. For example, it drove my Kermie crazy when I called him my little smiddledyums, and I did not like his habit of chewing flies. So both of us gave a little, and now my little smiddledyums and moi are even happier.

What should a woman do until her true love comes along?

Circulate, circulate, circulate!

Can a woman ever really know what is in the heart of a man?

No, never. She can only guess. That is life. The good news is, men can only guess what is in the heart of a woman. And *they* are lousy guessers.

Should a woman have secrets she keeps from the man she loves?

Should chocolates have cherry centers? Should satin pillows have fluffy stuffing?

How can a woman be in love with a man and still not be vulnerable?

It is impossible. You must take risks, and, oui, you can suffer terribly. This moi knows. Before I met my Kermie, I had many stormy, tempestuous relationships, and they often ended sadly. But although that is all in the past, I would do it again without hesitation. A woman must take chances. Faint heart ne'er won fair frog.

What do men look for in a woman?

They look for someone feminine, sweet, intelligent, and demure. They look for a companion with understanding and compassion. They look for that certain flair, that *je ne sais pas*. They look for style, substance, and sweep. They look for a full, generous figure coupled with a deep, smoldering gaze. And then, alas, just when they have found it, I must tell them that I am spoken for.

Success

Your Career—It's in Your Closet

I cannot tell you how many young ladies write to me and say, Miss Piggy, if *only* I could find an interesting, rewarding career like yours—one with excitement, travel, and glamour.

Goodness knows, I sympathize with their predicament. I moiself spent many years engaged in assorted occupations which were frankly unworthy of a person of my many gifts, before I stumbled on this one basic secret of success: if you're properly attired, you're hired. And if you're not, I don't care how "qualified" you may be—it will be a case of "clothes, but no cigar!"

What very few people realize is that there are only a handful of professions that require any actual knowledge or skill. (I will have a list of these risky problem areas a little later on.)

Dressed to Skill

Look around you. Do you ever see a brain surgeon in a tutu or a high-priced attorney in gingham? Of course not. Persons working in the more challenging fields know that it is expected of them to dress appropriately.

After all, how would you react if the electrician you sent for to fix the lights showed up in a clown suit? Or if the pilot on your next flight wore a gorilla costume? Clothing lends confidence, and confidence is essential to successful performance in any endeavor, whether you are a superstar (well, I guess that is a bit unlikely) or an elevator inspector or a nuclear engineer.

And what is true of the impression you make on the public is even more true when it comes to the all-important job interview. Now, anyone with taste can dress well for a social occasion and make a very favorable impression. But if, for example, you wish to pursue a career in the interesting construction field, you certainly do not want to show up for an interview in an outfit that features a stylish beret, a beaded bag, an understated suit, and stiletto heels. A clipboard, a nice little lunchbox, and a hat a brick will bounce off of are far more effective in demonstrating your basic grasp of your chosen vocation.

All very well, I can hear you protesting, but, Miss Piggy, what good is it if I can dress like a chemist (demure white coat, a fairly simple hairstyle, a few really good pens in your pocket) or a psychiatrist (conservative skirt—light plaid or tweed—plain white or solid color pastel blouse, a simple necklace, and a pretty notepad with a nice cover) when I don't know the difference between a Bunsen burner and some nutbar with fritzophrenia?

Well, the simple fact is that everyone in just about every occupation picked up everything he needed to know "on the job." Let's face it, everyone was taught just about the same things in school, and although most of it was quite fascinating, none of it is of the slightest bit of use, practically speaking, in a day-to-day job. When I go to the dentist, I don't ask him to tell me what he knows about the Edict of Aunts or why Charlemagne Bonaparte lost the Battle of Honeydew to the Melons. And just like everybody else in his profession, for the first few weeks, he spent his time wandering around asking what all the different nasty little tools were for and where the button was that fills the paper cup with pink mouthwash and how to get all those old magazines.

Of course, no matter what profession you choose to enter, you are going to have to pick up a few bits of jargon, like "I hereby issue a writ of hocus-pocus," or "Redemnify this convertible debenture and put white sidewalls on it and shine its coupons," or "Give me full power in the flaps and vents, and lower the tassels." And you will have some catching up to do, because in some professions, like law, many people have been to schools where they were taught useful phrases, how much to charge, and—most important—what to wear. There is no doubt about it –you must have the gift of gab, but it is the gift of garb that will provide you with that vital first break.

If You Have the Rags, You Will Get the Riches!

In the next few pages, I have modeled a few typical examples of career apparel to give you an idea of how to evaluate various kinds of occupations. After careful study of my "gown for renown" principles, and a few weeks spent considering available positions which match your fashion aspirations and investing in your vestments, you should be ready to put on your get-up and go!

THE LAW

Classic, elegant suits and robes with handsome leather accessories (bags and cases), but little opportunity for dynamic dress expression or career wardrobe growth thanks to fusty, stick-in-the-mud legal tradition; acceptable lunch hour, but restaurants and shopping in vicinity of courthouses are invariably mediocre; very booksy office decor with diploma accents, but too much paper in a most unpleasant shade of yellow.

WIFE AND MOTHER

Limitless selection of clothing styles, except during maternity periods; proximity to kitchen permits a high level of luncheon leisure; home decor is entirely a matter of personal taste although ill-conceived decorating suggestions from husband may spoil overall effect.

WIMBLEDON WINNER

Cute, athletic-type frock with some room for color expression appearing in
recent years, but full fashion display only available during prize acceptance;
limited lunching periods due to thoughtless match schedules and antiquated
"training" rules; locker rooms almost always smell like buses, lack adequate
privacy, and feature bomb-shelter-type appointments.

INTERIOR DECORATOR

Necessity of demonstrating flawless taste to potential clients requires a constantly updated, well-chosen wardrobe; lunch is often "on the go," which is poor for the digestion, but fortunately the need to keep up with the latest restaurant designs requires regular lengthy visits to the best places; since career is largely spent in showrooms, antique stores, and fashionable homes, actual office is relatively unimportant but should certainly have a supersoft full-length chaise longue for resting feet, munching bonbons, and leafing through fancy magazines.

MODEL

Unlimited access to an infinite variety of dramatic clothing styles at the cutting edge of high fashion; dreary diets can cast a pall on luncheon opportunities; generally pleasant surroundings in which to work characterized by constant attention from beauticians and makeup artists and a closet the size of an office (instead of the other way around!).

"UNDERGROUND" RESTAURANT CRITIC

Continually shifting garment repertoire with the accent on clever disguises
(the need for a steady development of new ruses ensures great latitude for
experimentation with novel styles); lunch *is* the occupation; since restaurants
are the workplace, surroundings vary from dingy basement munch-hovels with
waxy wine bottles and electrified pictures of the Bay of Naples on velvet to
chic bistros with tasteful appointments.

PRIMA BALLERINA

Enchanting, romantic costume and some opportunity for fashion advancement depending on roles; excessive practice requirements and unfortunate craze for underfed "sylph" look tends to limit luncheon potential; dressing rooms vary from bright, airy roomettes to dank cubicles with soapstone mop sinks and sweaty brick walls.

Choosing a Fashionable Future

When you are trying to decide on a career, make sure that the profession that has captured your fancy has the essential things you are looking for. Don't get sidetracked early on by minor considerations like prestige, starting salary, and various benefits.

Here is a handy checklist for evaluating how well your career will "wear" in years to come:

1. Does the career of your choice involve a strict style of dress that you will still have to be happy with five years from now? Ten? If so, make certain that you really look good in it, because if your tastes change later, there is little that you are going to be able to do about it except grin and wear it.

2. Does your chosen career offer an opportunity for genuine fashion growth? Take a look at the people who occupy the top jobs in the profession which has caught your eye. Has success in their field put them "in the mink" or does some silly tradition or question of ethics mean that people in their line of work who dress up are in for a dressing down?

3. Does your career choice provide for a proper lunch hour? I just cannot emphasize this aspect of prospective employment too strongly. Some otherwise very desirable occupations have absurdly short periods set aside for luncheon—in some cases, as little as one hour or even less! It is worth considering that in an average thirty-five-year career, you should expect to spend no less than three solid years eating lunch (and shopping, or whatever—"lunch" is quite properly a very loose term).

4. Does the career you have selected make possible imaginative and elegant office decor? Try to get a look at the offices of the leaders of your profession. Are they cramped, sparse little dungeons, cluttered with messy papers, bulky office machinery, and depressing metal cabinets, or are they cozy, comfortable living rooms with soft chairs, pretty pictures, and plush carpets?

✤ TOP BUSINESS EXECUTIVE

Conservative clothing on the whole, but with essentially "bottomless" closet not only permitted but expected by stockholders and board members; occupation is basically conducted over one continuous lunch; lavish office decor, usually involving a suite of rooms, with exciting additional design opportunities to add personal touch (curtains, plants, wall sconces, etc.) to assembly lines and the interiors of little jet planes.

Travel

Being a superstar, I have to travel quite a bit, both in our own country and overseas. Consequently, I have learned just about everything there is to know about making a trip as comfortable and enjoyable as possible. If you abide by the simple precepts I have listed below, you will have the benefit of my many years of travel experience.

Miss Piggy's Rules to Leave By

1. When to Pack. Never pack the night before. If your mind is on going to bed, you are very likely to pack your pillow, your night table, and ten pairs of pajamas and forget something important, like a dozen extra hats or those nice fur-lined booties.

2. Early-Morning Departures. Never begin a trip of any kind before noon. If you do, you will be in such a mental fog that you will wind up going to the airport to catch a bus and arriving there with your dirty laundry hamper, your vacuum cleaner, and none of your luggage.

3. What to Pack. The basic rule here is, when in doubt, pack it. It has been clearly documented that many times in the earth's history, there have been sudden, drastic changes of climate. What if you are in Florida without your furs, and there is a very quick little ice age?

4. How to Pack. Having a great many individual suitcases, hatboxes, valises, etc., is like traveling with a large though somewhat sluggish family. In any event, you should never take more pieces of luggage than one helpful person can carry for you all by himself without making two trips.

5. Departure Time. There is simply no point at all in spending hours and hours hanging around airports, bus terminals, and train stations with nothing to do but take little pictures of yourself in those automatic photo booths. Anyway, they will always hold the plane for you. After all, if they leave you behind, they are just going to have to come back and get you, so they would really rather wait.

6. Snacks. Depending on the length of your trip, you should provide

yourself with a good supply of teensy tidbits to munch on. *Never* rely on the food available at transport terminals, particularly if it comes out of a machine. You have no idea what goes on in there.

7. Tickets and Traveling Documents. These should be kept in a handy place where you can check them several hundred times.

8. Reading Matter. Bring copies of your favorite magazines, plus several light, entertaining books (*not* some dreadful best-selling novel with words like *Crash, Doom,* and *Horror* written all over the cover).

9. Travel Arrangements. Whenever possible, avoid airlines which have anyone's first name in their titles, like Bob's International Airline or Air Fred.

10. Companions. I, of course, usually travel with Kermit, but if you're traveling alone, beware of seatmates who by way of starting a conversation make remarks like, "I just have to talk to someone—my teeth are spying on me" or "Did you know that squirrels are the devil's oven mitts?"

11. Accommodations. Generally speaking, the length and grandness of a hotel's name are an exact opposite reflection of its quality. Thus, the Hotel Central will prove to be a clean, pleasant place in a good part of town, and the Hotel Royal Majestic-Fantastic will be a fleabag next to a topless bowling alley.

12. Restaurants. Eating places with live plants in their windows are always good. Restaurants with peppermills the size of fire extinguishers and big red menus with the entrées spelled with "f's" instead of "s's" are always expensive. Italian restaurants with more than 120 entrées are always disappointing. There are no good French restaurants in states which have a "K" in their names. (New Yorque is the exception that proves the rule, whatever that means.)

Foreign Travel

Many of these general rules apply to travel abroad as well as at home, but there are some important differences, mostly in money, weights and measures, and language. Actually, it does not take long to get the knack of converting dollars into francs, fiats, paellas, and dustmarks, or ounces, degrees, and miles into telegrams, thermostats, and speedometers. What is a bit tricky, though, is converting English into a foreign language. Let me show you my basic method.

You have to be going to a pretty awful place if getting there is half
the fun, but you can make your journey a lot more pleasant with a
little bit of planning.

Foreigners have a very roundabout and confused way of saying things.
Here's how I cope. I am in a restaurant, and I want a piece of the delicious
chocolate cake I see displayed on a shelf. "Personality who bringulates les
munchables," I call, summoning the waiter. When he arrives, I give my
order. "If it does you please, transportez [trans-por-TAY] to moi's tablette
one gigantical smithereeni de that chocolate cakefication avec as immense
a velocité [vee-luss-ee-TAY] as possible." And there you are!

There are just a few final things you should keep in mind:

Continental breakfasts are very sparse, usually just a pot of coffee or
tea and a teensy roll that looks like a suitcase handle. My advice is to go
right to lunch without pausing.

Public telephones in Europe are like our pinball machines: They **are**
primarily a form of entertainment and a test of skill rather than a means
of communication.

Bon voyage!

Your Questions Answered

Dear Miss Piggy,

All of my plants, which were once so nice and green, have turned brown and died. What should I do?

Bereft

Dear Bereft,

That is truly sad. And green is such a pretty color. . . . But cheer up. Plants are just like lamps. You plug them in and they turn right on. When they stop working, just unplug them, throw them away, and plug in another.

♥ ♥ ♥

Dear Miss Piggy,

Whenever I cook spaghetti, it always gets all tangled up into clumps. What am I doing wrong?

Frustrated

Dear Frustrated,

I am not sure, but you might try a light cream rinse, followed by a quick once-over with a blow-dryer.

♥ ♥ ♥

Dear Miss Piggy,

For some reason, my garden this year produced a bumper crop of cabbages, and I don't know what to do with them all. Are there any good cabbage recipes?

Green Thumb

Dear Green Thumb,
No.

Dear Miss Piggy,

Is there anything you can do with the ends you cut off asparagus stalks? Asparagus isn't cheap, and it seems like you're throwing half of it away.

Thrifty

Dear Thrifty,

Well, I guess you could dye them and thread a string through them and hang the whole mess up somewhere, or maybe just stick a lot of tooth-picks in them, and make . . . look, is it really that important? Can't you just stick them in a bag and then when you have forgotten all about it, just toss them out?

♥ ♥ ♥

Dear Miss Piggy,

I have a couple of old-fashioned sash windows that have a large gap where the two halves meet. When there's a wind, they rattle all night, and in winter there is a terrible draft. What can I do?

Rattled

Dear Rattled,

An interesting problem. You know what you might try? Take a hand-ful of cut-off asparagus spear ends and work them into the cracks. Not only will this eliminate that annoying rattle and stop up the draft, but it will give you something useful to do with the otherwise wasted halves of what is, after all, a rather costly vegetable.

♥ ♥ ♥

Dear Miss Piggy,

My hinges squeak, and the sound is driving me bananas. Is there anything I can do?

Unhinged

Dear Unhinged,

Try hammering a prune into them. If the problem persists, add honey.

♥ ♥ ♥

Dear Miss Piggy,

If a base runner is struck by a foul ball that bounces off a wall into fair territory and hits him, is he out?

Bleacher Bum